Houghton Mifflin Harcourt Scho

Ohio Achievement Test and Practice

Use with *Ohio HSP Math* and
Houghton Mifflin Harcourt Math Expressions

Includes:

- **Practice Tests in Achievement Test Format**
- **Standards Practice**
- **Vocabulary and Skills Practice**
- **Problem Solving**

Grade 2

HOUGHTON MIFFLIN HARCOURT

1 2 3 4 5 6 7 8 9 10   018   17 16 15 14 13 12 11 10 09

Contents

Being a good test-taker is like being a good problem solver. When you answer test questions, you are solving problems. Remember to **UNDERSTAND, PLAN, SOLVE,** and **CHECK.**

UNDERSTAND

· Read the problem.

· Think about the question.

· Look for numbers and find important words.

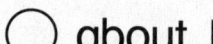 Mason took 10 pictures at Yosemite National Park. Jackie took 8 pictures of it. About how many pictures do they have in all?

○ about 1

○ about 10

○ about 20

 The word **about** tells you to estimate.

- Look at any pictures, tables, and graphs.
- You may need to remember another math skill.
- What math skill do you need to use?
- Do you need to write a number sentence?

2 Use the tally chart to answer the question.

Theme Park Rides We Like

water slide	⩘⩘⩘⩘⩘
roller coaster	⩘⩘⩘⩘⩘ |||
bumper cars	|||

How many children like the water slide best?

○ 2
○ 5
○ 7

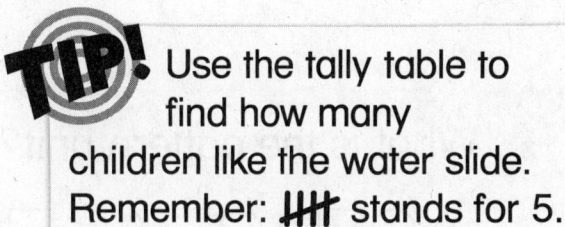

TIP! Use the tally table to find how many children like the water slide. Remember: ⩘⩘⩘⩘⩘ stands for 5.

- Follow your plan.

- Is your answer one of the answer choices?

- If not, re-read the problem and solve it again.

- Change your plan if it isn't working. Try a different strategy.

- Make sure you solved all the steps.

3 What is the pattern unit?

△○□△○□△○□

○ △△△

○ △♡□

○ △○□

TIP! Find choices that you know are not right. The second choice is not right because there is no heart in the pattern in the question.

- Look for any mistakes.
- Did you answer the question that was asked?
- Check your computation in a different way.

4 Jessica wrote the numbers below on her paper.

6   7   9

Which number when used to write a doubles fact equals 14?

○ 6
○ 7
○ 9

TIP! Check your work. Look at your answer choice. Does it match the question that was asked?

1. **NO1** **Which symbol makes the sentence true?**

43 ◯ 53

◯   ◯   ◯

<   >   =

2. **G5** **Which shows a line of symmetry?**

◯   ◯   ◯

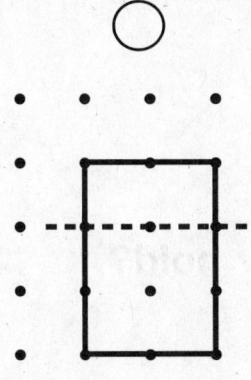   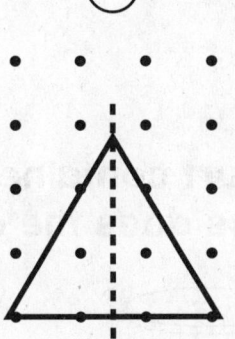   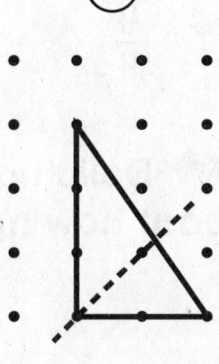

3. **NO10** **What is the difference?**

$$\begin{array}{r} 12 \\ -\ 3 \\ \hline \boxed{} \end{array}$$

◯   8

◯   9

◯   10

Go to next page ▶

4. **NO5** Linus shaded the circle.

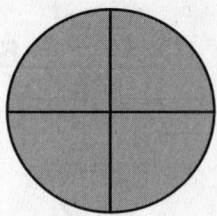

What fraction of the rectangle did he shade?

○ $\frac{1}{4}$

○ $\frac{3}{4}$

○ $\frac{4}{4}$

5. **M7** Delia has a yogurt container.
About how many cups does the container hold?

1 cup

○ about 2 cup

○ about 4 cups

○ about 6 cups

Go to next page ➤

6. **DAP2** Use the line plot.

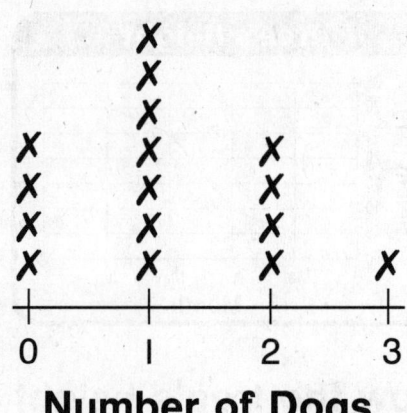

Number of Dogs

What number of dogs do the <u>most</u> children have?

○ 1 dog

○ 2 dogs

○ 3 dogs

7. **NO8** Brett gives 15 markers to 3 friends. Each friend gets the same number of markers. How many markers does each friend get?

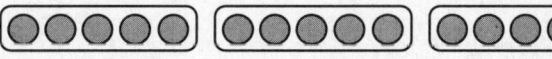

○ 3 markers

○ 4 markers

○ 5 markers

Go to next page

8. **A7** Use the line graph.

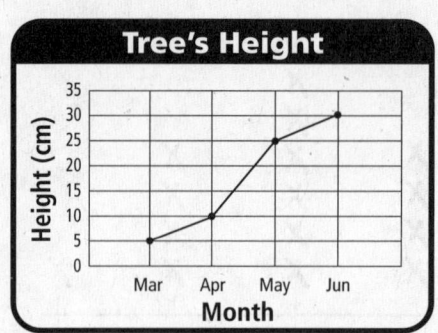

Which describes how the tree's height changed
from March to May?

○ It grew 20 centimeters taller.

○ It grew 10 centimeters taller.

○ It grew 5 centimeters taller.

9. **NO2** Which number is odd?

○ 10

○ 12

○ 13

Go to next page ➜

10. 🔘M3 **Ed's family went on vacation for 1 week. Which amount of time is the same as 1 week?**

○ 7 days

○ 60 minutes

○ 12 months

11. 🔘NO6 **Cora has 8 toy cars. She gives 3 of the cars to her brother. Which number sentence tells how many toy cars Cora has left?**

○ $8 - 3 = 5$

○ $8 - 4 = 4$

○ $8 + 3 = 11$

12. 🔘M6 **Which tool is best to find the length of the yarn?**

〰〰〰〰〰〰〰〰〰

○ a scale

○ a ruler

○ a thermometer

Go to next page ➡

13. **M4** **Which clock shows the same time?**

○ 2:15

○ 2:30

○ 2:45

14. **NO9** **What is the missing sum?**

$$6 + 9 = 15$$
$$9 + 6 = \boxed{}$$

○ 3

○ 15

○ 17

15. **DAP1, DAP6** Tyler took a survey of his friends. He used tally marks to show their answers.

Our Favorite Weekend Activities	
Activity	**Tally**
read	ⅢⅢ
hike	ⅢⅢ Ⅰ
bike	ⅢⅠ

Which question did Tyler ask to get the answers in his tally table?

○ How often do you read on the weekend?

○ What is your favorite weekend activity?

○ What did you do this weekend?

16. **NO7** Which multiplication sentence is shown?

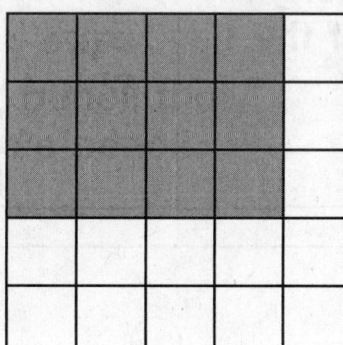

○   ○   ○

$3 \times 4 = 12$ $4 \times 5 = 20$ $3 \times 3 - 9$

Go to next page

17. **G3** Which object is shaped like a cube?

○   ○   ○

18. **NO3** What is the total value?

○   ○   ○

16¢   19¢   21¢

19. **M5** Use an inch ruler.
What is the length of the chalk
to the nearest inch?

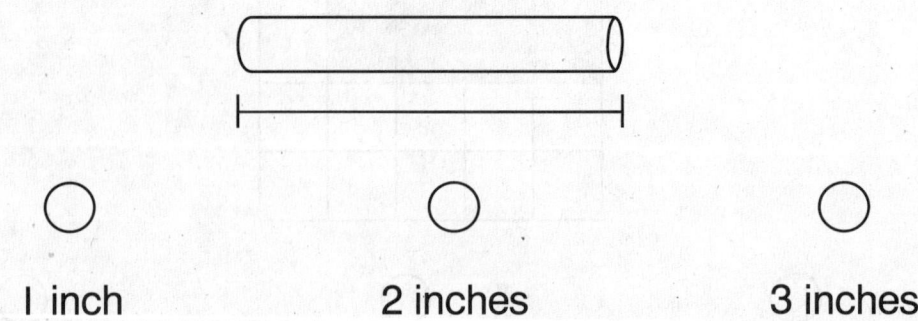

○   ○   ○

1 inch   2 inches   3 inches

Go to next page

20. **MI** Which unit is best to measure the length of a stapler?

    ◯ inch

    ◯ foot

    ◯ yard

21. **NO13** Jacob has 39 marbles.
His brother has 28 marbles.
About how many more marbles
does Jacob have than his brother?

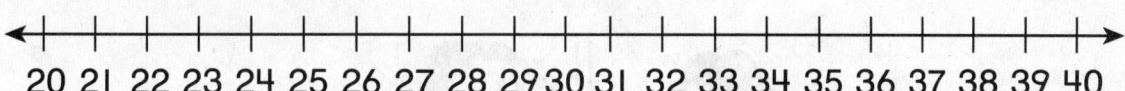

20 21 22 23 24 25 26 27 28 29 30 31 32 33 34 35 36 37 38 39 40

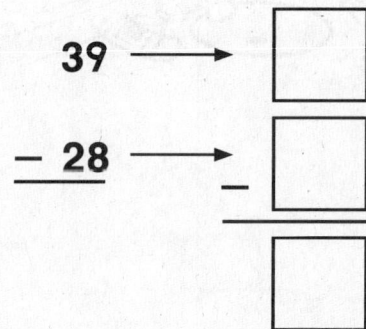

39 →

− 28 →

   ◯   ◯   ◯

about 10   about 20   about 30

Go to next page

22. **DAP7** **What are the possible outcomes for the spinner?**

○ gray, white, and black

○ gray and white

○ black and gray

23. **MI** **About how long does it take to brush your teeth?**

○ about 2 minutes

○ about 20 minutes

○ about 2 hours

Go to next page ➤

10

24. **A4** Alyssa and her friends have some beads. They make the table below to show how many beads each friend has.

Our Beads	
Name	**Number of Beads**
Darla	28
Maria	36
Isabelle	29

How many beads do Darla and Maria have in all?

○ 44 beads

○ 54 beads

○ 64 beads

25. **NO4** Nathan buys a snack that costs $1.00. Which coins show $1.00?

○

○

○

Go to next page ➡

26. **DAP3** **Look at the point on the time line. Which would you most likely do at that time?**

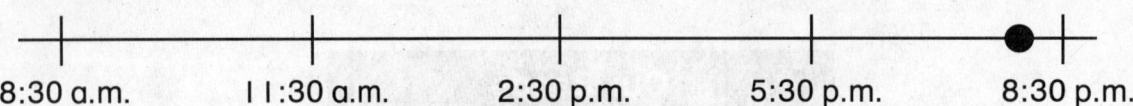

8:30 a.m.   11:30 a.m.   2:30 p.m.   5:30 p.m.   8:30 p.m.

○ eat lunch

○ wake up

○ go to sleep

27. **M2** **About how many liters does the container hold?**

○ about 2 liters

○ about 20 liters

○ about 200 liters

Go to next page ➤

28. **AI** Which pattern does the hundred chart show?

1	2	3	4	5	6	7	8	9	10
11	12	13	14	15	16	17	18	19	20
21	22	23	24	25	26	27	28	29	30
31	32	33	34	35	36	37	38	39	40
41	42	43	44	45	46	47	48	49	50
51	52	53	54	55	56	57	58	59	60
61	62	63	64	65	66	67	68	69	70
71	72	73	74	75	76	77	78	79	80
81	82	83	84	85	86	87	88	89	90
91	92	93	94	95	96	97	98	99	100

○ Count by twos.

○ Count by threes.

○ Count by fours.

29. **NO6** Margie had 4 balloons.
Her mom gave her some more balloons.
Now Margie has 10 balloons.
How many balloons did her mom give?

$$4 + ? = 10$$

○ 6 balloons

○ 8 balloons

○ 14 balloons

Go to next page ➤

30. I am a solid figure that rolls and slides.
Which solid figure am I?

○

○

○

31. **NO8** What division sentence does the number
line show?

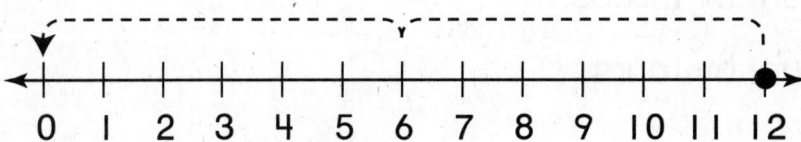

○   ○   ○

12 ÷ 6 = 2   12 ÷ 3 = 4   6 ÷ 3 = 2

32. **A2** What letter is missing from the pattern?

L M M N L M M N L M __ N

○   **L**

○   **M**

○   **N**

Go to next page ➡

33. **M3** **Ally is sick for 4 days.
Is this more than, less than,
or the same as 1 week?**

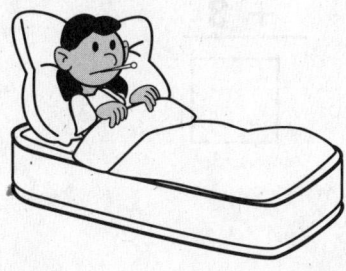

○ less than

○ more than

○ the same as

34. **M3** **What is the rule for the table?**

In	Out
0	1
2	3
4	5
6	7

○ Add 3.

○ Add 2.

○ Add 1.

Go to next page

35. **NO10** **What is the total sum?**

$$
\begin{array}{r}
3 \\
4 \\
+\ 3 \\
\hline
\end{array}
$$

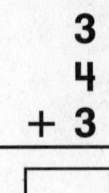

○ 9

○ 10

○ 11

36. **M1** **Which unit is best to measure the weight of the cherry?**

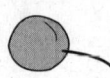

○ ounce

○ pound

○ meter

37. **A5** **What number completes the number sentence?**

$$2 + 8 = \boxed{} + 4$$

○ 4

○ 5

○ 6

Go to next page

38. **M4** **Which shows another way to write the time?**

◯   15 minutes after 4 o'clock

◯   45 minutes after 3 o'clock

◯   45 minutes after 2 o'clock

39. **DAP4** **Use the bar graph.**

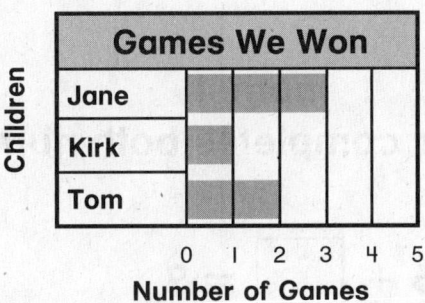

Who won the most games?

◯   Jane won the most games.

◯   Kirk won the most games.

◯   Tom won the most games.

Go to next page ➤

40. **G1** Which figure has 6 faces, 12 edges, and 8 vertices?

○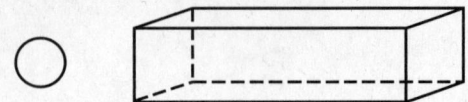

○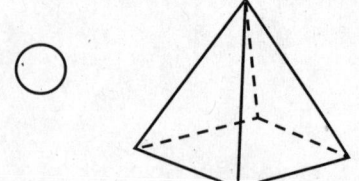

○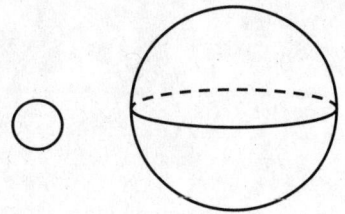

41. **A6** What number completes both number sentences?

$6 + \boxed{} = 9$

$9 - 6 = \boxed{}$

○ 2

○ 3

○ 4

Go to next page →

42. **NO11** Jason has 26 baseball cards.
He buys 30 more baseball cards.
How many baseball cards does he have now?

○ 36 baseball cards

○ 46 baseball cards

○ 56 baseball cards

43. **G4** Which shows 2 congruent figures?

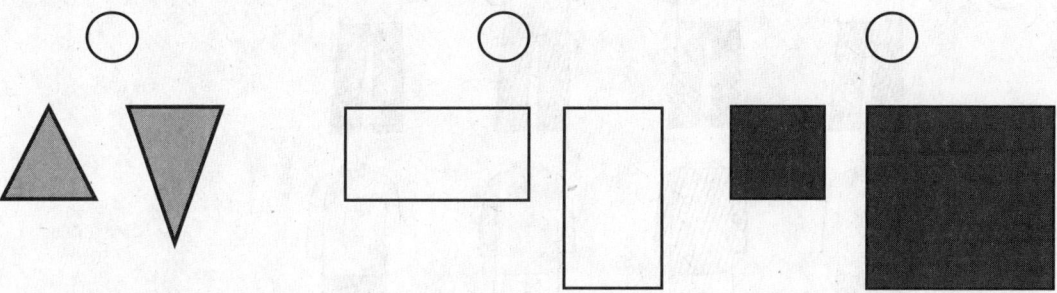

○   ○   ○

44. **NO12** Find two numbers in the box that
have ones digits that will make a ten.
Add the numbers. What is the sum?

216   170   138
312   407

○ $312 + 138 = 450$

○ $216 + 170 = 386$

○ $407 + 312 = 719$

Go to next page ➡

45. **DAP8** Liza uses 2 shirts and 2 pants to make outfits.

Which shows all the different outfits Liza can make?

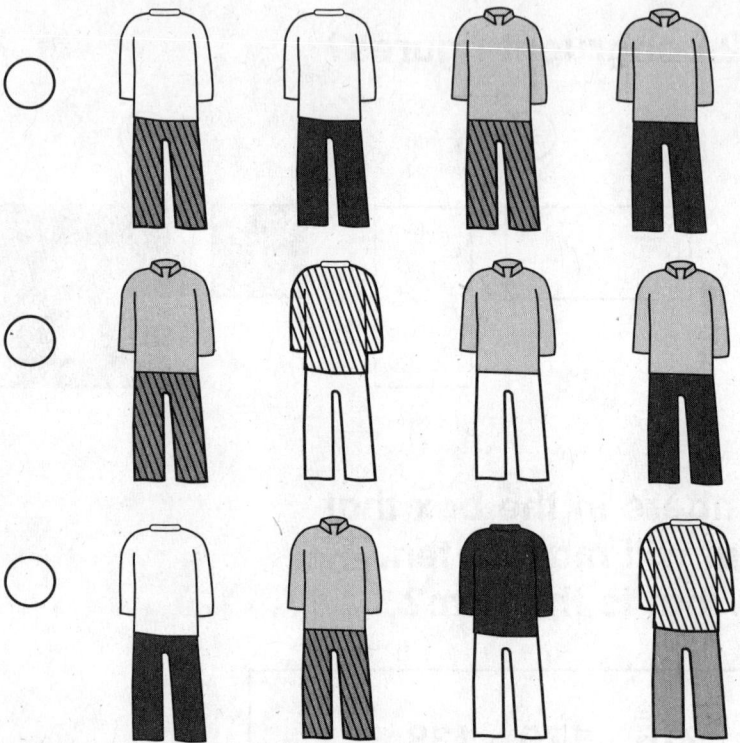

46. **NO3** Clark has 3 quarters.
He buys a package of pencils for 68¢.
Which shows Clark's change?

47. 🛡DAP5 **Use the picture graph.**

Favorite Fruits	
orange	🙂 🙂
apple	🙂 🙂 🙂 🙂
peach	🙂 🙂 🙂 🙂 🙂

Each 🙂 = 2 children.

Which statement is <u>not</u> true?

○ Four children chose orange.

○ Four children chose apple.

○ Ten children chose peach.

48. 🛡NO5 **What fraction names the shaded part?**

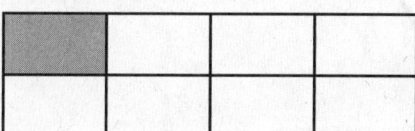

○ $\dfrac{1}{8}$

○ $\dfrac{1}{6}$

○ $\dfrac{1}{5}$

49. 🛡G3 **Which solid figure has 6 faces that are all squares?**

○   ○   ○

cone   pyramid   cube

Go to next page ➡

50. G2 **Ari has 5 triangles.**

**She combines the sides to make a new figure.
Which new figure might Ari make?**

○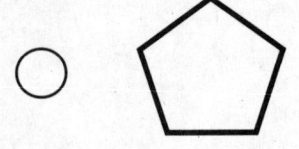

○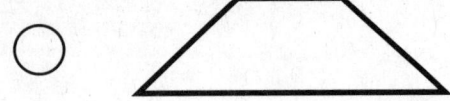

○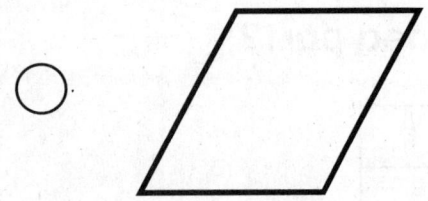

51. A5 **What number will complete
the number sentence?**

$$6 - \boxed{} = 2 + 2$$

○ 1

○ 2

○ 3

Go to next page ➡

22 Ohio Mathematics Achievement Test Practice

52. **NO3** Colin has:

He buys:

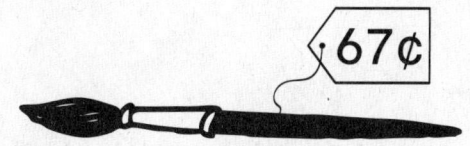

67¢

Draw coins to show Colin's change.

Go to next page ➜

53. M4 **Shana gets on the bus at 8:10 every morning.**

Draw the minute hand to show the time that Shana gets on the bus.

Then write the time Shana gets on the bus in another way.

_____ minutes after _____ o'clock

1. **◖MI** **About how long will it take to make a lunch?**

- ◯ about 10 hours
- ◯ about 10 minutes
- ◯ about 100 minutes

2. **◖A3** **What is the rule for the table?**

In	Out
0	5
1	6
2	7
3	8

- ◯ Add 4.
- ◯ Add 5.
- ◯ Add 6.

Go to next page ⮞

3. **NO7** Which multiplication sentence does the array show?

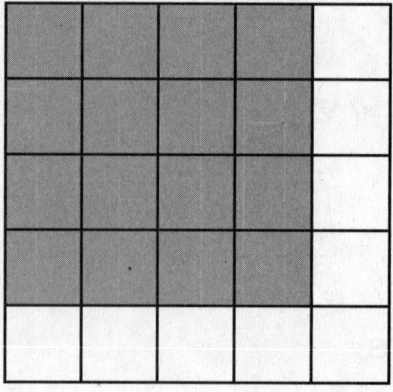

 $2 \times 4 = 8$

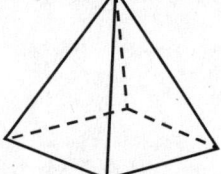 $4 \times 3 = 12$

 $4 \times 4 = 16$

4. **GI** Which figure has 5 faces, 8 edges, and 5 vertices?

 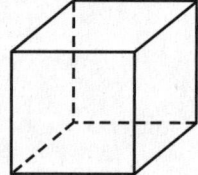

 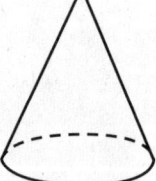

Go to next page ➡

5. **M4** **Which shows a way to write the time?**

○ 30 minutes after 4 o'clock

○ 30 minutes after 5 o'clock

○ 30 minutes after 6 o'clock

6. **G3** **Which object is shaped like a cone?**

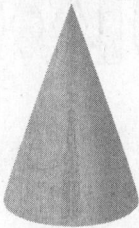

○

○

○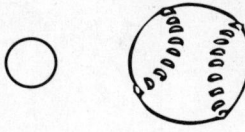

Go to next page ➜

7. **NO8** What division sentence does the number line show?

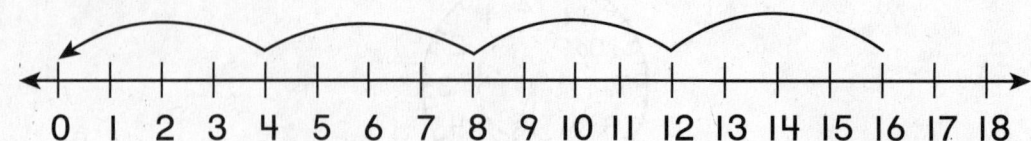

○ $16 \div 2 = 8$

○ $8 \div 4 = 2$

○ $16 \div 4 = 4$

8. **A2** What is the missing piece of the pattern?

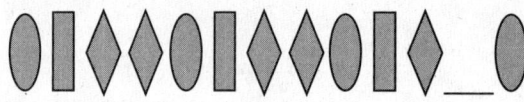

9. **NO3** Greg has 1 dollar.
He buys a bookmark for 93¢.
Which shows Greg's change?

○

○

○

Go to next page ➤

10. **M7** How many cups will the container hold?

1 cup

○ about $\frac{1}{2}$ cup   ○ about 2 cups   ○ about 4 cups

11. **NO5** George shades the square.

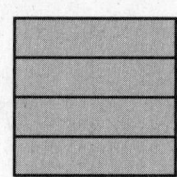

What fraction of the square does he shade?

○ $\frac{1}{4}$ ○ $\frac{3}{4}$ ○ $\frac{4}{4}$

12. **DAP3** Look at the point on the time line.
Which would you most likely do at that time?

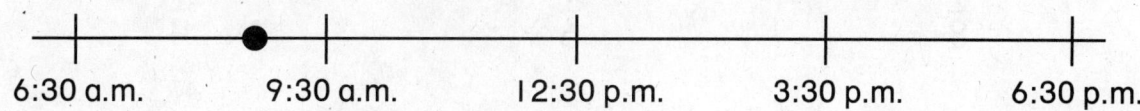

6:30 a.m.   9:30 a.m.   12:30 p.m.   3:30 p.m.   6:30 p.m.

○ go to school

○ eat lunch

○ go to sleep

Go to next page

13. **NO6** Charlie has 10 crackers.
He gives 6 of them to his friend.
Which number sentence tells how
many crackers Charlie has left?

◯   ◯   ◯

$10 - 6 = 4$ $10 - 4 = 5$ $6 + 10 = 16$

14. **NO10** What is the difference?

$$9 - 2 = \boxed{}$$

◯   5

◯   6

◯   7

15. **NO5** What fraction names the shaded part?

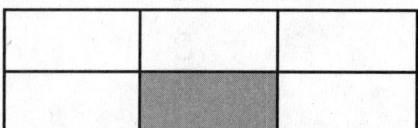

◯   ◯   ◯

$\dfrac{1}{8}$ $\dfrac{1}{6}$ $\dfrac{1}{4}$

Go to next page ➡

16. **M2** **About how many liters can the container hold?**

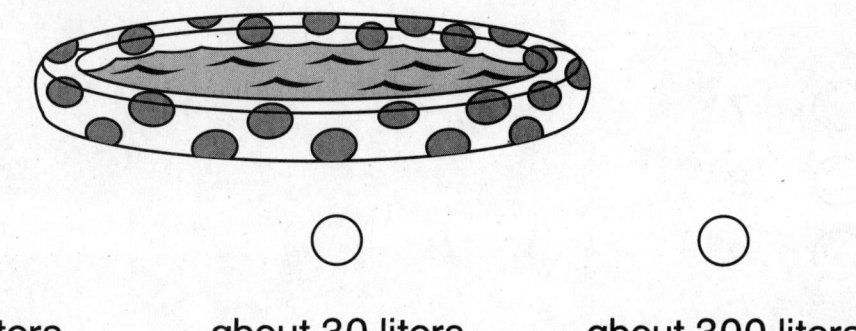

○ about 3 liters   ○ about 30 liters   ○ about 300 liters

17. **M6** **Erik wants to know how much the pear weighs. Which tool should he use?**

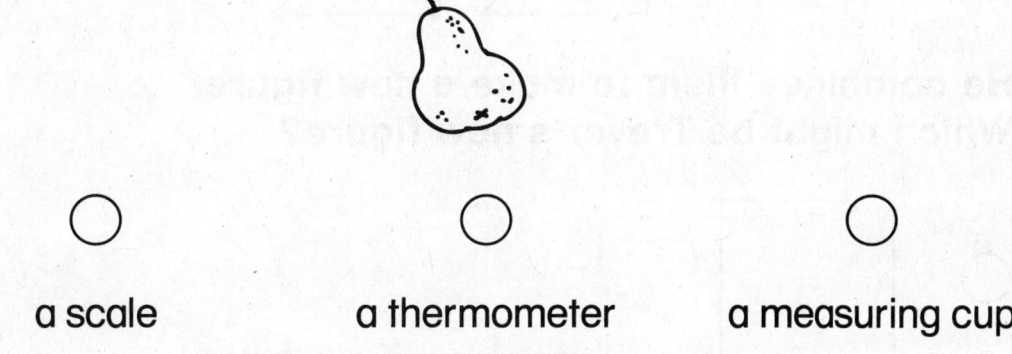

○ a scale   ○ a thermometer   ○ a measuring cup

18. **M3** **Sydney rode her bike for 1 hour. Which amount of time is the same as 1 hour?**

○ 1 day   ○ 60 minutes   ○ 12 months

Go to next page

19. 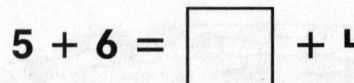 **What number will complete the number sentence?**

$$5 + 6 = \boxed{} + 4$$

- ○ 7
- ○ 8
- ○ 9

20. **G2 Trevor has two triangles.**

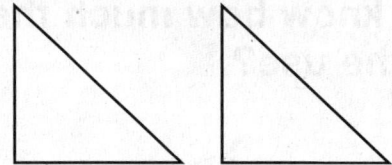

He combines them to make a new figure. Which might be Trevor's new figure?

- ○
- ○
- ○

Go to next page ➡

21. **A4** Laney and her friends have raisins.
They make a table to show how
many raisins each child has.

Our Raisins	
Name	**Number of Raisins**
Laney	38
Alexis	42
Marlo	19
Kirsti	27

How many raisins do Laney
and Marlo have in all?

○ 47 raisins

○ 57 raisins

○ 69 raisins

22. **NO8** Sam gives 8 orange pieces to 2 friends.
Each friend gets the same number of pieces.
How many orange pieces does each friend get?

 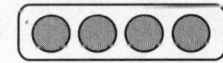

○ 2 pieces

○ 4 pieces

○ 6 pieces

Go to next page ➡

23. **DAP4** **Use the bar graph.**

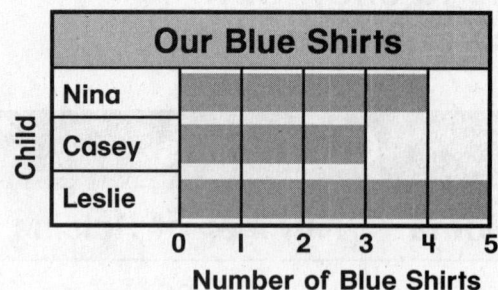

Our Blue Shirts

| Child | Nina | Casey | Leslie |

Number of Blue Shirts
0   1   2   3   4   5

Who has the most blue shirts?

○   Nina has the most blue shirts.

○   Casey has the most blue shirts.

○   Leslie has the most blue shirts.

24. **M3** **Sally's family lived in France
for 12 months.
Is this more than, less than,
or the same as 1 year?**

○   more than

○   less than

○   the same as

Go to next page

25. **G1** **I am a solid figure.**
    I slide but do not roll.
    I have 6 sides.
    What solid figure am I?

   ○    ○    ○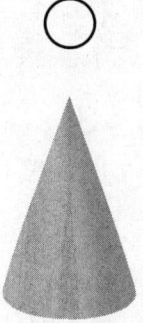

26. **N09** **What is the missing sum?**

   $$5 + 7 = 12$$

   $$7 + 5 = \boxed{}$$

   ○   12
   ○   13
   ○   14

27. **M5** **Use an inch ruler. What is the length of the crayon to the nearest inch?**

   ○   1 inch
   ○   3 inches
   ○   5 inches

Go to next page ➤

28. A6 **What number completes both number sentences?**

$$5 + \square = 9$$

$$9 - 5 = \square$$

- ○ 3
- ○ 4
- ○ 5

29. G5 **Which shows a line of symmetry?**

○ 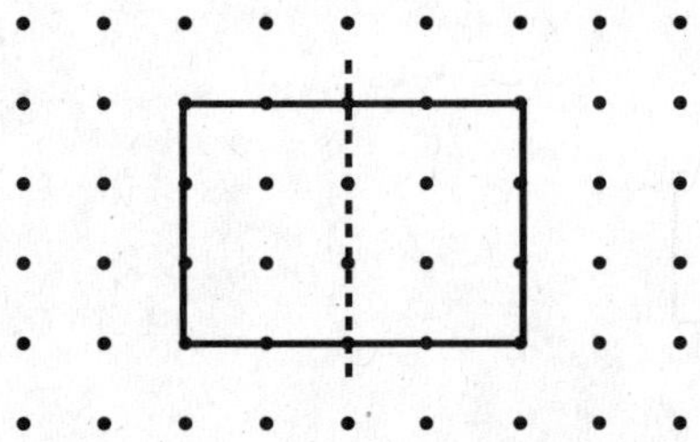

○ 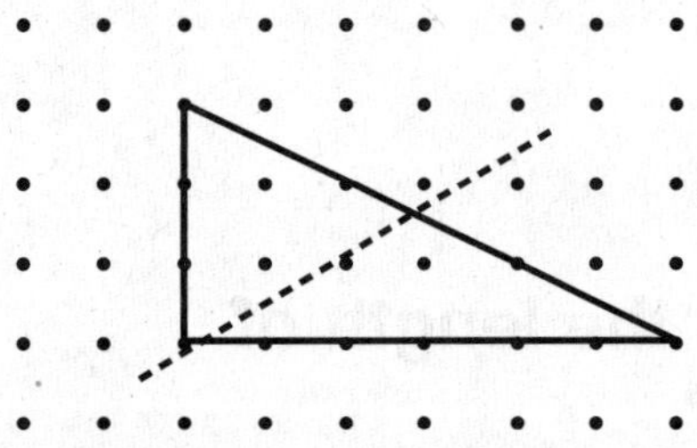

○ 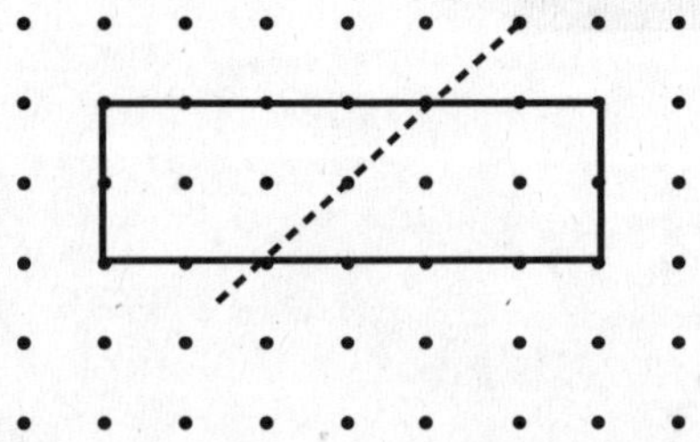

Go to next page

30. **G3** Which solid figure has some faces that are rectangles?

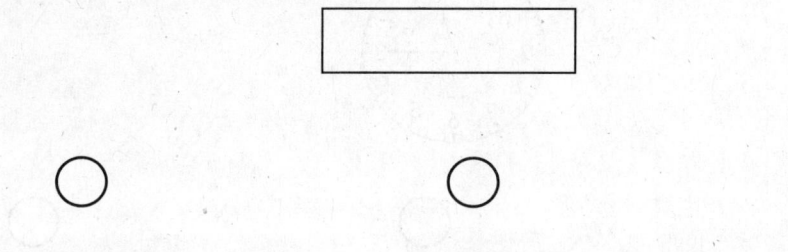

◯ sphere   ◯ cone   ◯ rectangular prism

31. **NO6** Kyle had 8 flowers.
Then Julie gave him some more flowers.
Now Kyle has 12 flowers.
How many fllowers did Julie give Kyle?

$$8 + ? = 12$$

◯ 3 flowers   ◯ 4 flowers   ◯ 5 flowers

32. **MI** Which unit would be best to measure the weight of the paper clips?

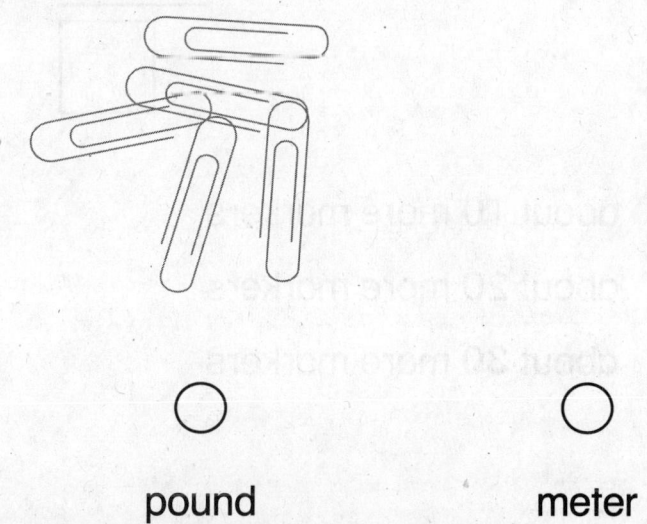

◯ ounce   ◯ pound   ◯ meter

Go to next page →

33. **M4** **Which clock shows the same time?**

○ 12:15   ○ 12:30   ○ 1:15

34. **NO13** **Sean has 28 markers.**
Amanda has 11 markers.
About how many more markers
does Sean have than Amanda?

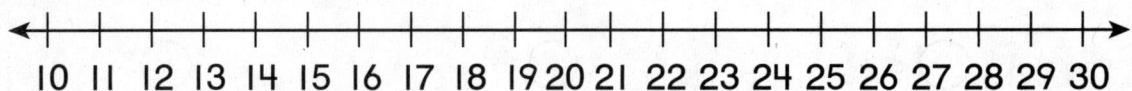

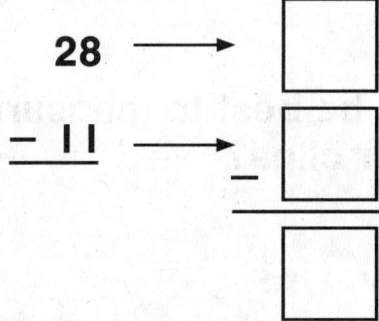

○ about 10 more markers

○ about 20 more markers

○ about 30 more markers

Go to next page

35. **DAP7** **What are the possible outcomes for the spinner?**

○ gray

○ white and gray

○ white

36. **G4** **Which shows congruent figures?**

○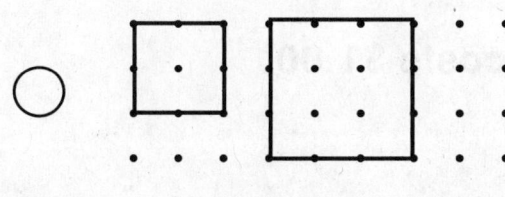

○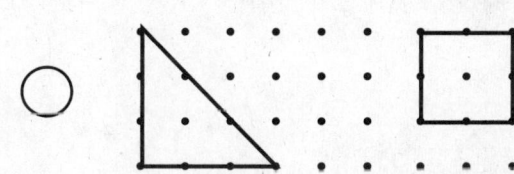

○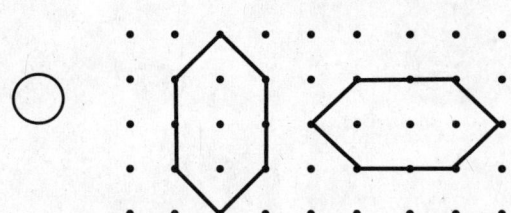

Go to next page

37. **MI** Which unit is best to measure the length of the house?

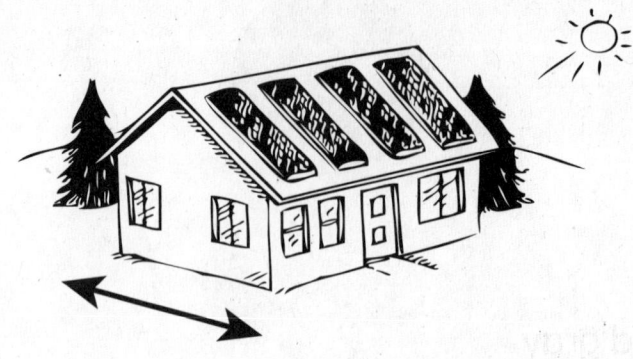

○ inch

○ foot

○ yard

38. **NO4** Andrea buys a drink that costs $1.00. Which coins show $1.00?

○

○

○

Go to next page →

39. **DAP5** **Use the picture graph.**

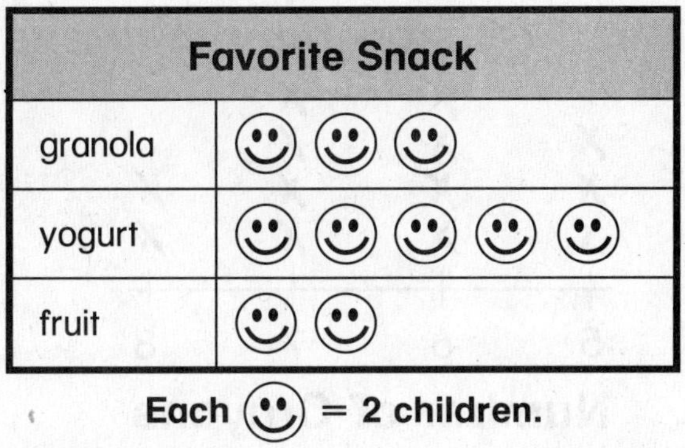

Favorite Snack	
granola	☺ ☺ ☺
yogurt	☺ ☺ ☺ ☺ ☺
fruit	☺ ☺

Each ☺ = 2 children.

Which statement is true?

○ Six children chose granola.

○ Five children chose yogurt.

○ Two children chose fruit.

40. **NO2** **Which number is even?**

○ 11

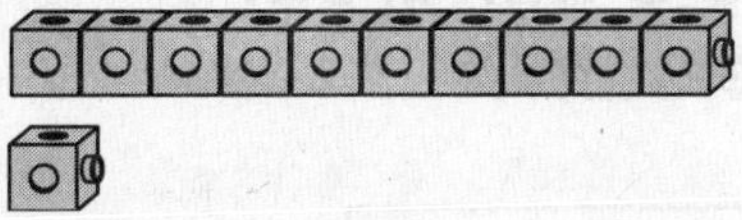

○ 12

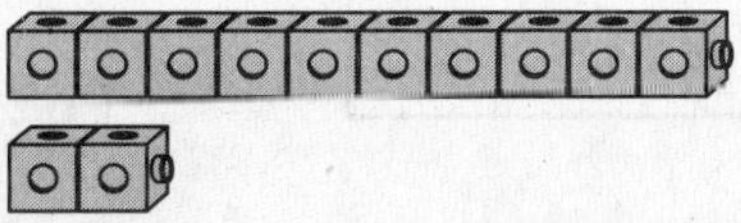

○ 13

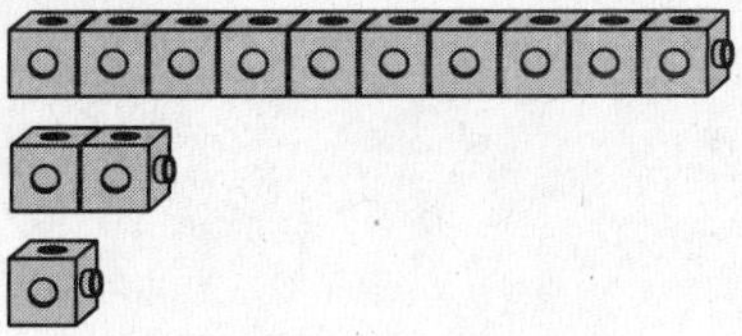

41. **DAP2** Use the line plot.

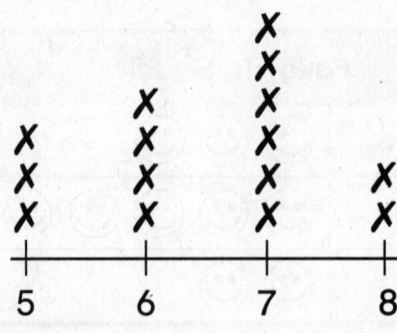

Number of Crayons

What number of crayons do the <u>most</u> children have?

○ 6 crayons

○ 7 crayons

○ 8 crayons

42. **NO12** Find two numbers in the box that have tens digits that will make a hundred. Add the numbers. What is the sum?

430	208	382
	560	270

○ $382 + 208 = 590$

○ $560 + 208 = 768$

○ $430 + 270 = 700$

Go to next page

43. **AI** **What pattern does the hundred chart show?**

1	2	3	4	5	6	7	8	9	10
11	12	13	14	15	16	17	18	19	20
21	22	23	24	25	26	27	28	29	30
31	32	33	34	35	36	37	38	39	40
41	42	43	44	45	46	47	48	49	50
51	52	53	54	55	56	57	58	59	60
61	62	63	64	65	66	67	68	69	70
71	72	73	74	75	76	77	78	79	80
81	82	83	84	85	86	87	88	89	90
91	92	93	94	95	96	97	98	99	100

◯ Count by twos.

◯ Count by fives.

◯ Count by tens.

44. **NO3** **Ella has 3 quarters. She buys a card for 62¢. Which shows her change?**

◯

◯

◯

Go to next page →

45. **DAP1, DAP6** Riley took a survey
of his classmates. He used tally marks
to show their answers.

Books We Like	
Kind	**Tally**
funny	⊦⊦⊦⊦ |||
mystery	||||
adventure	|||

**Which survey question did Riley ask
to get the answers in the tally table?**

○ What kind of books can you buy?

○ What kind of books are in the library?

○ What kind of books do you like to read?

46. **NO1** **Which symbol makes the sentence true?**

38 ☐ 34

○ <

○ >

○ =

Go to next page

47. **A7** **Use the graph.**

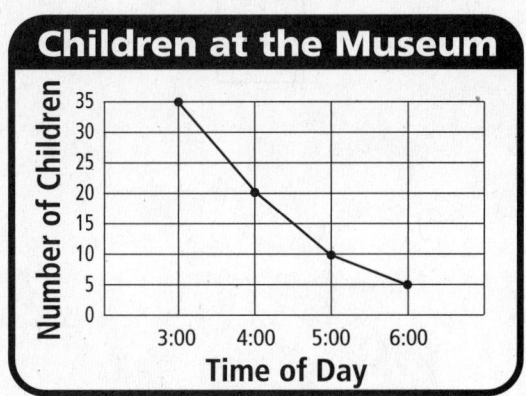

Children at the Museum

Number of Children

Time of Day

Which tells how the number of children changed from 3:00 to 6:00?

○ There were more children at 4:00.

○ There were fewer children at 3:00.

○ There were fewer children at 6:00.

48. **NO11** **Ryan has 34 marbles in a bucket. He adds 40 more marbles to the bucket. How many marbles are in the bucket now?**

$$34 + 40 = \boxed{}$$

○ 64 marbles

○ 74 marbles

○ 84 marbles

Go to next page

49. **NO10** **What is the sum?**

$$7 + 7 = \boxed{}$$

○ 13

○ 14

○ 15

50. **G1** **What is the name of the solid figure?**

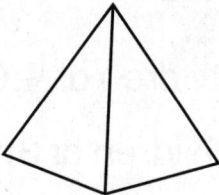

○ pyramid

○ cone

○ cylinder

51. **A5** **What number will complete the number sentence?**

$$12 - \boxed{} = 3 + 4$$

○ 5

○ 6

○ 7

Go to next page

52. ▸DAP7 **The table shows the colors of the marbles in Eva's bag.**

Marbles in the Bag	
Color	Number
blue	4
red	6
green	3
pink	4

Use the data in the table to make predictions.

Which color is Eva more likely to pull—blue or red?

_____

Which color is Eva less likely to pull—green or pink?

_____

Which two colors is Eva equally likely to pull?

_____

Go to next page ➡

53. **NO3** Jack has 1 quarter, 2 dimes,
1 nickel, and 3 pennies.

55¢

Granola Bar

Does Jack have enough money to buy the
granola bar? Write <u>yes</u> or <u>no</u>.

_____

Draw and label Jack's coins.
Then write the total value.

_____

STOP

1. **NO4** Jenny buys a pen that costs $1.00.
   Which coins show $1.00?

   ○

   ○

   ○

2. **M2** Gina has a pitcher of lemonade.
   About how many liters can the pitcher hold?

   I liter

   ○ about 2 liters
   ○ about 20 liters
   ○ about 200 liters

Go to next page ➔

3. **G3** Which object is shaped like a cylinder?

   ○

   ○

   ○

4. **A4** David and his friends have toy cars. They make a table to show how many toy cars each child has.

Our Toy Cars	
Name	Number of Toy Cars
David	19
Hector	28
Robert	37
Rita	22

How many toy cars do Hector and Rita have in all?

○ 40 toy cars

○ 50 toy cars

○ 65 toy cars

Go to next page

5. **NO5** **What fraction names the shaded part?**

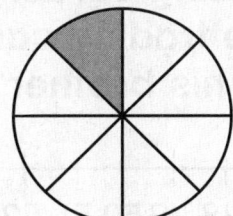

○ $\frac{1}{8}$

○ $\frac{1}{6}$

○ $\frac{1}{5}$

6. **NO5** **Annabell shaded the triangle.**

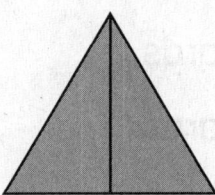

What fraction of the triangle did she shade?

○ $\frac{1}{4}$

○ $\frac{1}{2}$

○ $\frac{2}{2}$

Go to next page ▶

7. **NO13** Caleb has 57 trading cards.
His brother has 41 trading cards.
About how many more trading cards
does Caleb have than his brother?

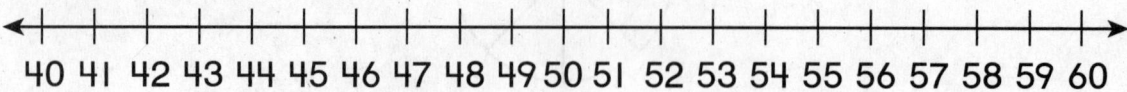

40 41 42 43 44 45 46 47 48 49 50 51 52 53 54 55 56 57 58 59 60

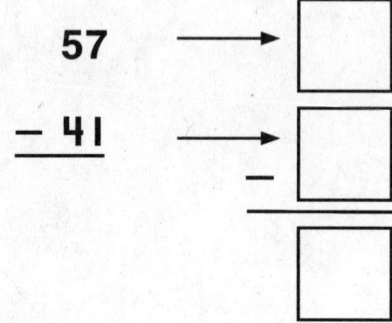

57 →

− 41 →

−

○ about 10 trading cards

○ about 20 trading cards

○ about 30 trading cards

8. **A5** What number will complete
the number sentence?

$$8 + 7 = \square + 4$$

○ 11

○ 12

○ 13

Go to next page ▶

9. 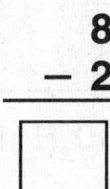 **NO10** **What is the difference?**

$$
\begin{array}{r}
8 \\
- 2 \\
\hline
\boxed{}
\end{array}
$$

○ 4

○ 5

○ 6

10. **DAP1, DAP6** **Amy took a survey of her friends. She used tally marks to show their answers.**

Places We Like	
Place	**Tally**
library	卌 II
museum	卌
pool	卌 III

Which question did Amy ask to get the answers in the tally table?

○ What do you do when you go to the library?

○ What place do you like to go to?

○ How often do you go to the pool?

Go to next page ➡

11. **NO8** **What division sentence does the number line show?**

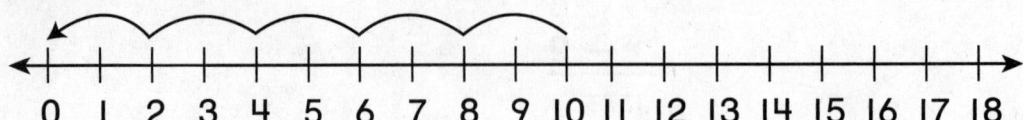

0 1 2 3 4 5 6 7 8 9 10 11 12 13 14 15 16 17 18

○ $10 \div 2 = 5$

○ $18 \div 9 = 2$

○ $8 \div 2 = 4$

12. **DAP5** **Use the picture graph.**

Favorite Juice	
apple	☺ ☺ ☺
pear	☺ ☺
grape	☺ ☺ ☺ ☺ ☺

Each ☺ = 2 children.

Which statement is not true?

○ Six children chose apple juice.

○ Four children chose pear juice.

○ Five children chose grape juice.

Go to next page ➤

13. **M3** **Tim learned to ride his bike in 3 days. Is this more than, less than, or the same as 1 week?**

    ○   ○   ○

more than   less than   the same as

14. **G1** **Which figure rolls but does not slide?**

    ○   ○   ○

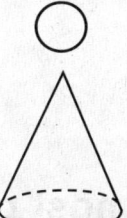
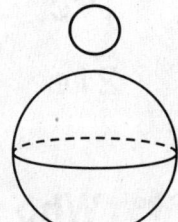

15. **M3** **Mr. Lee lived in another country for 1 year. Which amount of time is the same as 1 year?**

○ 7 days

○ 60 minutes

○ 52 weeks

Go to next page ➡

16. **A6** What number completes both number sentences?

$$4 + \boxed{} = 12 \qquad 12 - 4 = \boxed{}$$

○　　　　　　　○　　　　　　　○

6　　　　　　　7　　　　　　　8

17. **NO3** What is the total value?

○　17¢

○　19¢

○　21¢

18. **DAP4** Who scored the most points?

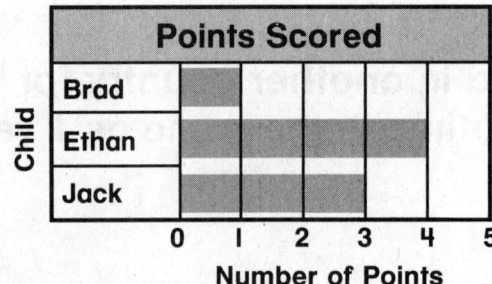

○　Brad scored the most points.

○　Ethan scored the most points.

○　Jack scored the most points.

Go to next page ➡

19. **A5** What number will complete
the number sentence?

$$12 - \boxed{} = 6 + 1$$

○ 4

○ 5

○ 6

20. **G4** Which shows congruent figures?

○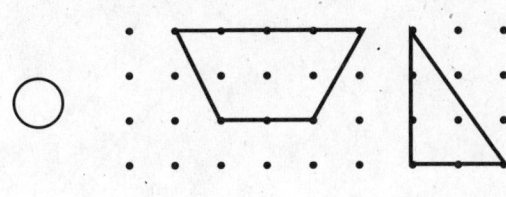

○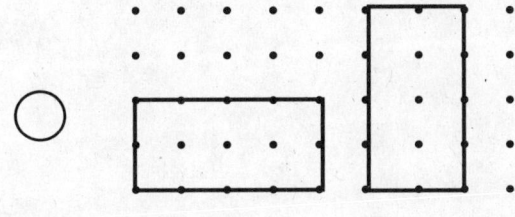

○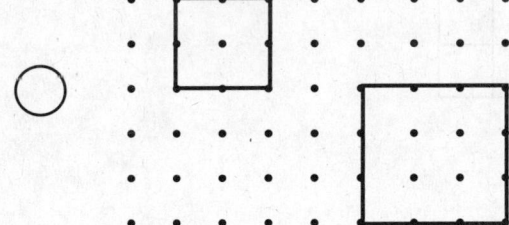

Go to next page ➤

21. **MI** Which unit is best to measure the length of a frog?

○ inch   ○ foot   ○ yard

22. **NO2** Which number is even?

○ 11

○ 13

○ 14

23. **NO7** Which multiplication sentence is shown?

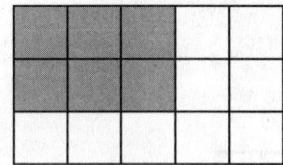

○ 2 × 3 = 6

○ 2 × 4 = 8

○ 3 × 4 = 12

Go to next page ➤

24. **NO6** Hanna has 14 peanuts.
She gives 4 of them to her brother.
Which number sentence tells how
many peanuts Hanna has left?

○   18 − 4 = 14

○   14 − 4 = 10

○   14 + 4 = 18

25. **A7** Use the line graph.

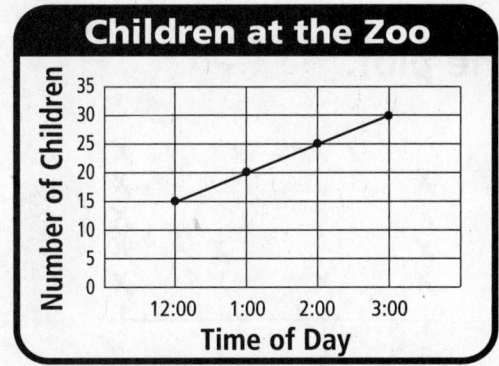

Which tells how the number of children
changed from 12:00 to 3:00?

○   There were more children at 12:00.

○   There were more children at 3:00.

○   The number of children did not change.

Go to next page ➤

26. **NO12** **Find two numbers in the box that have ones digits that will make a ten. Add the numbers. What is the sum?**

| 107 | 213 | 611 |
| 418 | 358 |

○ $418 + 358 = 776$

○ $358 + 611 = 969$

○ $107 + 213 = 320$

27. **DAP2** **Use the line plot.**

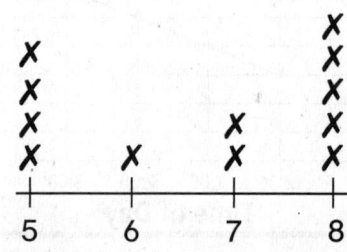

Number of Birds Seen

What number of birds did the <u>most</u> children see?

○   6 birds

○   7 birds

○   8 birds

Go to next page ➡

28. **NO3** **Ben has:**

He buys a drink for 55¢.
Which shows his change?

○

○

○

29. **DAP3** **Look at the point on the time line.**
Which would you most likely
do at that time?

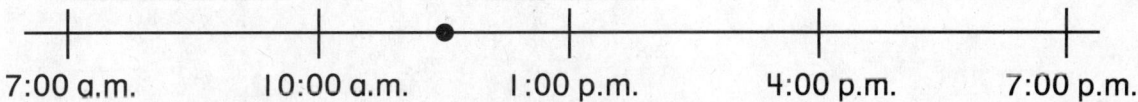

7:00 a.m.   10:00 a.m.   1:00 p.m.   4:00 p.m.   7:00 p.m.

○ go to sleep

○ eat lunch

○ eat dinner

Go to next page ➡️

30. 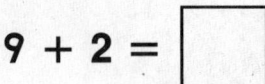 **What is the sum?**

$$9 + 2 = \boxed{}$$

○   ○   ○

9   10   11

31. 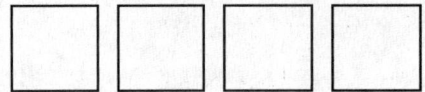 **Jonathan has 4 squares.**

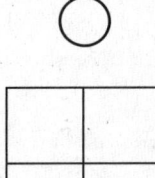

**He combines the squares to make a new shape.
Which might be Jonathan's new shape?**

○   ○   ○

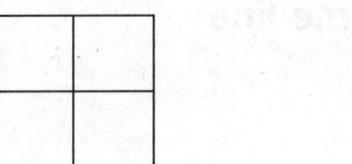 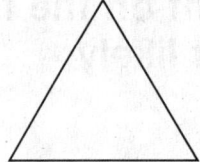 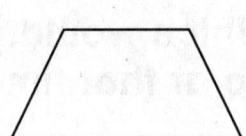

32. **What is the missing sum?**

$$4 + 8 = 12$$

$$8 + 4 = \boxed{}$$

○   10

○   11

○   12

Go to next page ➡

33. **G5** **Which shows a line of symmetry?**

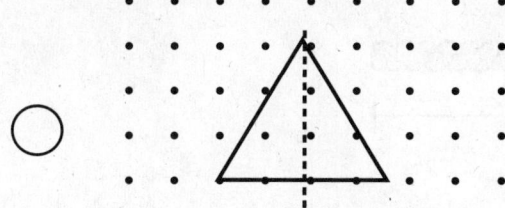

⭕

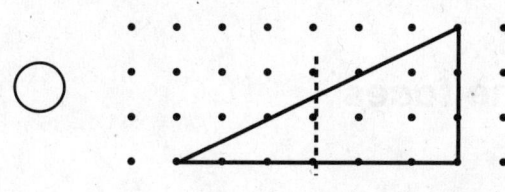

⭕

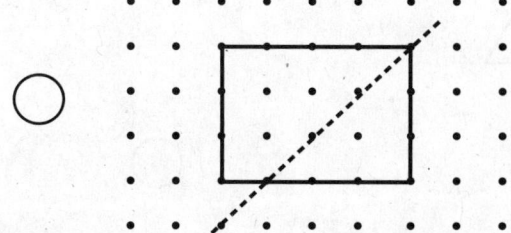

⭕

34. **NO11** **Kate has 21 buttons.**
She buys 20 more buttons.
How many ribbons does Kate have now?

$$21 + 20 = \boxed{}$$

⭕ 31 buttons

⭕ 41 buttons

⭕ 51 buttons

Go to next page ➜

35. M5 **Estimate. What is the length of the rope to the nearest inch?**

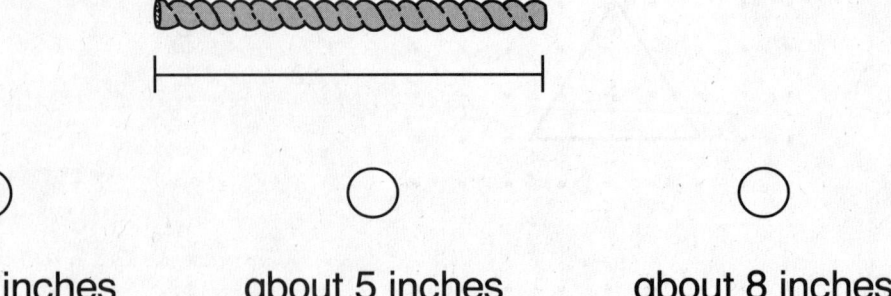

    ◯   ◯   ◯

about 2 inches   about 5 inches   about 8 inches

36. G3 **Which solid figure has some faces that are triangles?**

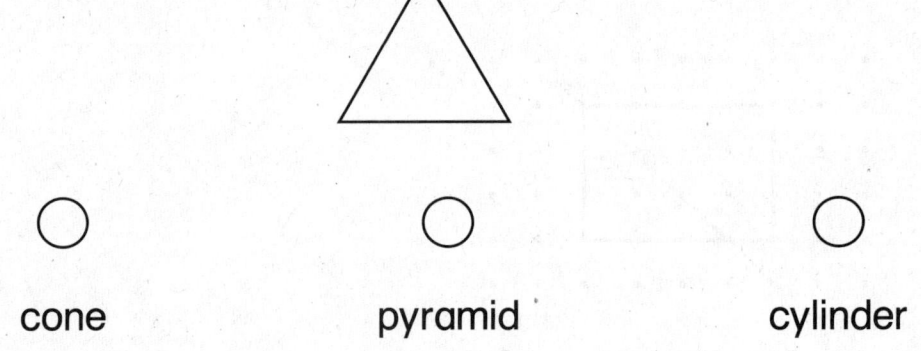

    ◯   ◯   ◯

cone   pyramid   cylinder

37. M7 **Violet has a large milk jug. About how many cups can the jug hold?**

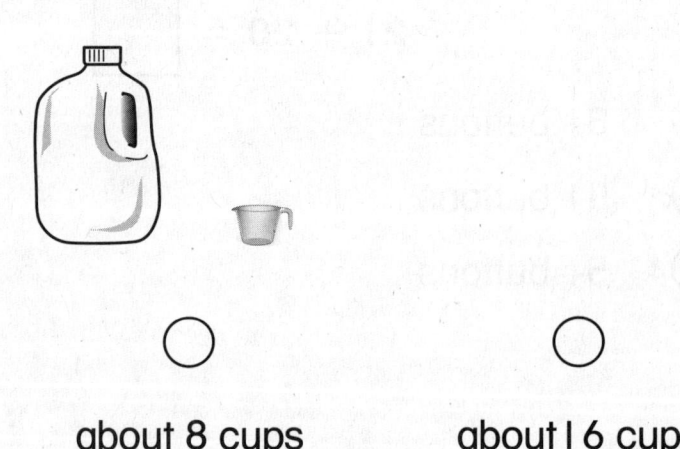

    ◯   ◯   ◯

about 4 cups   about 8 cups   about 16 cups

Go to next page →

38. **DAP8** Brent uses 2 shirts and
2 pants to make outfits.

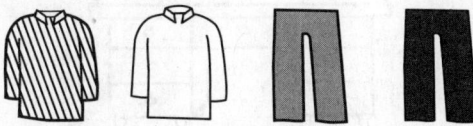

Which shows all the ways Brent can make outfits?

○

○

○

39. **NO1** **Which symbol makes the sentence true?**

29 ◯ 29

○ <

○ >

○ =

Go to next page ➡

40. **M1** Which unit is best to measure the weight of a desk?

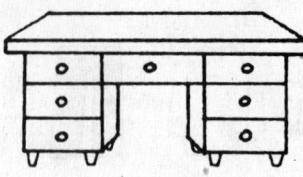

    ○   ○   ○

  ounce   pound   meter

41. **M4** Which clock shows the same time?

○   7:45

○   8:45

○   7:30

42. **M6** Ted wants to find out how hot his milk is. Which tool should he use?

    ○   ○   ○

a scale   a measuring cup   a thermometer

Go to next page

43. **A3** **What is the rule?**

In	Out
0	5
3	8
6	11
9	14

○ Add 1.

○ Add 3.

○ Add 5.

44. **NO8** **Dori gives 16 pencils to her 4 sisters.**
Each sister gets the same number of pencils.
How many pencils does each sister get?

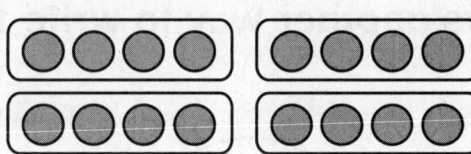

○ 3 pencils

○ 4 pencils

○ 5 pencils

Go to next page

45. ⬛**AI** **Which pattern does the hundred chart show?**

1	2	3	4	5	6	7	8	9	10
11	12	13	14	15	16	17	18	19	20
21	22	23	24	25	26	27	28	29	30
31	32	33	34	35	36	37	38	39	40
41	42	43	44	45	46	47	48	49	50
51	52	53	54	55	56	57	58	59	60
61	62	63	64	65	66	67	68	69	70
71	72	73	74	75	76	77	78	79	80
81	82	83	84	85	86	87	88	89	90
91	92	93	94	95	96	97	98	99	100

◯   Count by twos.

◯   Count by threes.

◯   Count by fives.

46. ⬛**M4** **Which shows another way to write the time?**

◯   40 minutes after 3 o'clock

◯   40 minutes after 2 o'clock

◯   40 minutes after 1 o'clock

Go to next page ➡

47. **DAP7** Which shows all the possible outcomes for the spinner?

⭘ white   ⭘ gray and black   ⭘ black and white

48. **NO6** Sam drew 9 pictures on Saturday.
He drew some more pictures on Sunday.
He drew 15 pictures in all.
How many pictures did Sam draw on Sunday?

$$9 + ? = 15$$

⭘ 6 pictures   ⭘ 8 pictures   ⭘ 24 pictures

49. **A2** What is the missing piece?

⭘ ⬛

⭘ ⬜(gray)

⭘ (striped)

Go to next page ➡

50. **MI** About how long will it take
to wash the dishes?

- ○ about 10 minutes
- ○ about 10 hours
- ○ about 2 hours

51. **GI** I am a solid figure with a curved face.
I roll and slide.
Which solid figure am I?

○

○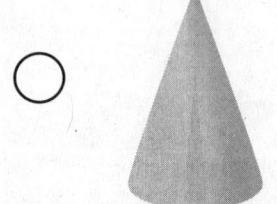

○

Go to next page ➡

52. ▶M5 **Cora has a pencil.**
She wants to use different units
to measure the length of the pencil.

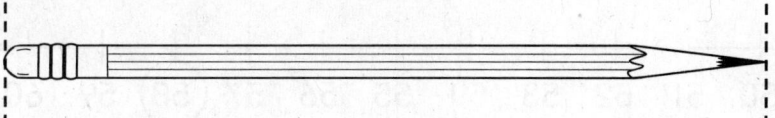

Use an inch ruler.

What is the length of Cora's pencil
to the nearest inch?

about _____ inches

Use a centimeter ruler.

What is the length of Cora's pencil
to the nearest centimeter?

about _____ centimeters

Draw a picture of a pencil that
is shorter than Cora's pencil.

Go to next page ▶

53. **NO1** **There are 58 children at a swimming pool. Are there about 50 children or about 60 children at the pool?**

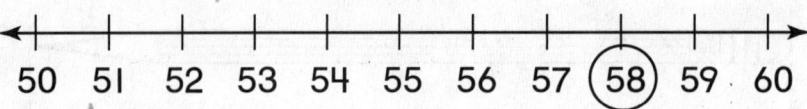

58 rounds to _____ .

So, there are about _____ children at the pool.

A group of 16 children leaves the pool. Now there are 42 children at the pool. Are there about 40 children or about 50 children at the pool?

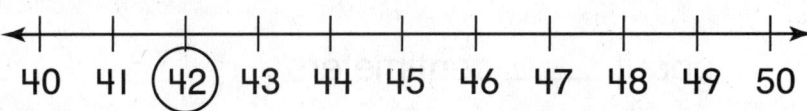

42 rounds to _____ .

So, there are about _____ children at the pool.

NO1 Use place value concepts to represent, compare and order whole numbers using physical models, numerals and words, with ones, tens and hundreds. For example, a. Recognize 10 can mean "10 ones" or a single entity through physical models and trading games. b. Read and write 3-digit numerals and construct models to represent each.

1. **Which statement is true?**

   ○ 347 > 364

   ○ 144 = 146

   ○ 243 < 254

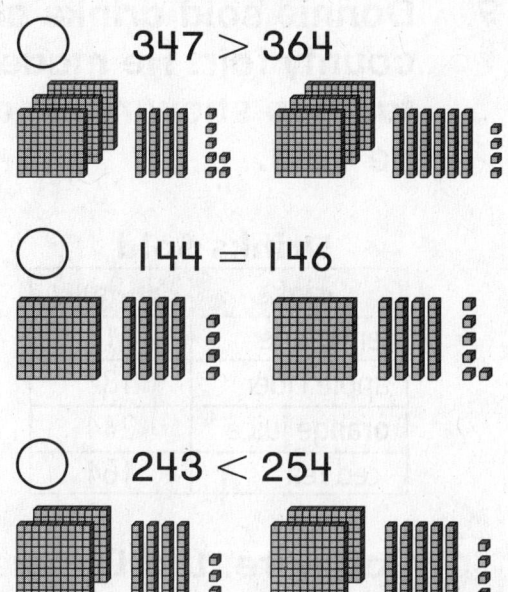

2. **The teacher asks Olga to write 913 in a different way. Which way can Olga write the number?**

   ○ 900 + 1 + 3

   ○ 391

   ○ 9 hundreds 1 ten 3 ones

3. **Which symbol makes the sentence true?**

   54 ◯ 64

   ○ <

   ○ >

   ○ =

4. **What is another way to show the number?**

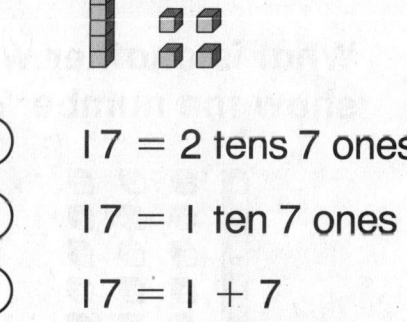

   ○ 17 = 2 tens 7 ones

   ○ 17 = 1 ten 7 ones

   ○ 17 = 1 + 7

5. Trenton has twenty-four fish in his aquarium. What is another way to write twenty-four?

○ 4 tens 2 ones

○ 2 + 4

○ 24

6. Which number will make the statement true?

$$35 < \boxed{} < 39$$

○ 34

○ 36

○ 40

7. What is another way to show the number?

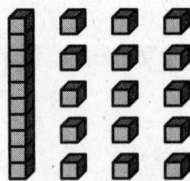

○ 1 ten 15 ones

○ 1 ten 5 ones

○ 2 tens 15 ones

8. Circle the value of the underlined digit.

3<u>8</u>1

300   30   3

9. Donnie sold drinks at the county fair. He made a table to show many drink he sold.

Drinks Sold

Drinks	Number
lemonade	217
apple cider	182
orange juice	244
iced tea	164

Compare. Did Donnie sell more lemonade or more orange juice at the county fair?

217 ◯ 244

Donnie sold more

_____

at the county fair.

NO2 **Recognize and classify numbers as even or odd.**

1. Mrs. Berg has 3 red folders, 2 blue folders, and 5 green folders on her desk.

   Which color folder does she have an even number of?

   ○ 3 red folders

   ○ 2 blue folders

   ○ 5 green folders

2. Which number is odd?

   ○ 12

   ○ 14

   ○ 17

3. Which number is even?

   ○ 15

   ○ 21

   ○ 24

4. Malia wants to sort her beads into an even number of groups.

   How many groups could she make?

   ○ 5 groups

   ○ 6 groups

   ○ 9 groups

5. Which number is odd?

   ○ 27

   ○ 28

   ○ 30

6. Which number is even?

   ○ 11

   ○ 26

   ○ 27

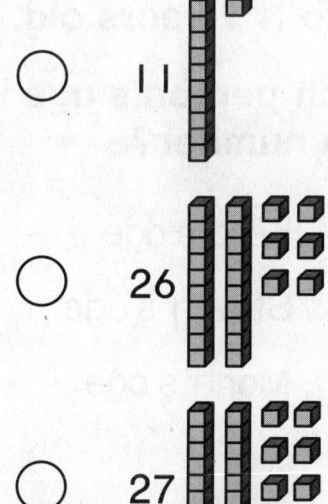

7. **Alexa has an even number of pets.**

    Which could show how many pets Alexa has?

    ○ 3

    ○ 4

    ○ 5

8. **Which number is odd?**

    ○ 9

    ○ 12

    ○ 18

9. **Kara is 8 years old. Steven is 7 years old and Marlo is 9 years old.**

    Which person's age is an even number?

    ○ Kara's age

    ○ Steven's age

    ○ Marlo's age

10. **Draw connecting cubes to show the number. Write even or odd.**

    28

    _____

11. **Justin has 5 cousins. Does he have an even number or odd number of cousins?**

    _____

12. **Katie has 14 marbles. Jenna has 15 marbles.**

    Does Katie or Jenna have an even number of flowers?

    _____

13. **Is 32 an even number or an odd number?**

    _____

Ohio Mathematics Achievement Test Practice

Name _____

NO3 Count money and make change using coins and a dollar bill.

1. **Which is true?**

○ 20¢ = 22¢

○ 17¢ > 12¢

○ 26¢ < 21¢

2. **Count the coins.**

What is the total value?

○ 87¢

○ 92¢

○ 97¢

3. **What is the total value?**

○ 86¢

○ 91¢

○ 96¢

4. **What is the total value?**

○ 27¢

○ 30¢

○ 32¢

5. **Which is a way to show 78¢?**

○

○

○

6. **Eve has I dollar. She buys a toy frog.**

Which shows her change?

○

○

○

7. **Count the coins. What is the total value?**

○ 27¢

○ 32¢

○ 37¢

8. **Compare. Write the total value of each group. Then write >, <, or =.**

_____ ◯ _____

9. **Julia draws I quarter and 3 dimes to show 55¢.**

What is a different way to show 55¢? Draw and label each coin.

NO4 Represent and write the value of money using the ¢ sign and in decimal form when using the $ sign.

1. **Which shows 75¢?**

○

○

○

2. **Count the coins. What is the total value?**

○ 78¢

○ 80¢

○ 82¢

3. **Count the coins. What is the total value?**

○ 96¢

○ 97¢

○ 99¢

4. **What is the total value?**

○ 55¢

○ 60¢

○ 65¢

5. **Tate buys a notebook that costs $1.00. Which coins show $1.00?**

○

○

○

6. **Jessie has 31¢ in her pocket. Which shows 31¢?**

○

○

○

7. **Count the coins.**

What is the total value?

○ 87¢

○ 92¢

○ 97¢

8. **Count the coins.**

What is the total value?

○ 27¢

○ 37¢

○ 39¢

9. **Draw and label dimes to show $1.00.**

10. **Count the coins. What is the total value?**

_____ ¢

NO5 **Represent fractions using words, numerals, and physical models.**

1. **What fraction of the square is shaded?**

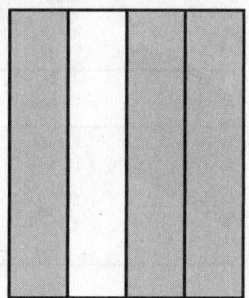

○ $\frac{1}{4}$

○ $\frac{2}{4}$

○ $\frac{3}{4}$

2. **What fraction names the shaded part?**

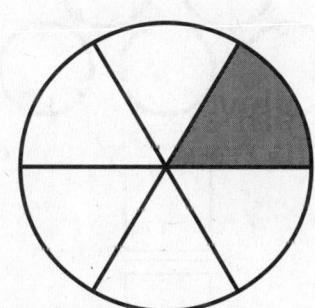

○ $\frac{1}{5}$

○ $\frac{1}{6}$

○ $\frac{1}{8}$

3. **Malia colored this rectangle.**

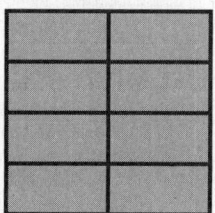

What fraction of the rectangle did she color?

○ $\frac{4}{4}$

○ $\frac{6}{6}$

○ $\frac{8}{8}$

4. **Which shows five sixths of a group shaded?**

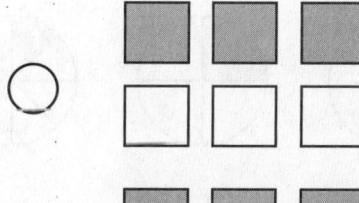

○

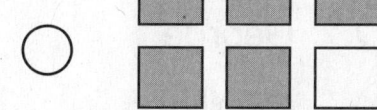

○

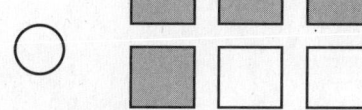

○

5. **Which shows two-thirds of the whole shaded?**

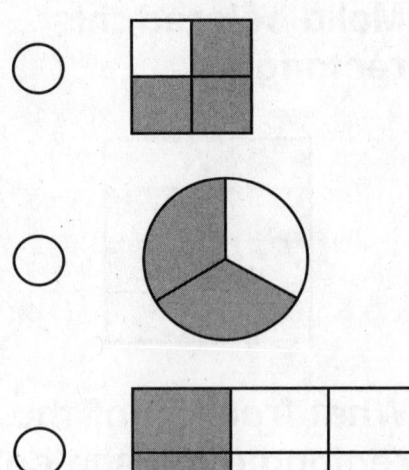

6. **Three peaches are the same size. George eats $\frac{1}{2}$ of a peach. Charlie eats $\frac{1}{4}$ of the second peach. Mason eats $\frac{1}{8}$ of the third peach. Who eats the most?**

◯ George

◯ Charlie

◯ Mason

7. **Is $\frac{1}{3}$ or $\frac{1}{6}$ greater? Color the fraction strips to compare. Circle the greater fraction.**

$$\frac{1}{3}$$

$$\frac{1}{6}$$

8. **Elijah has 5 marbles. Three-fifths of his marbles are green. Shade the green marbles. Write the fraction.**

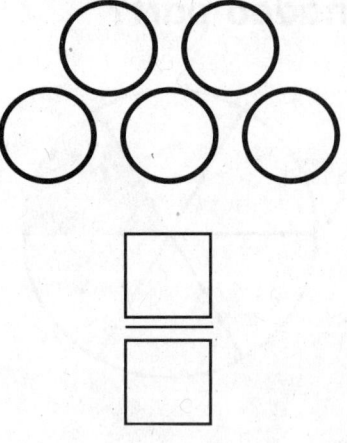

Name _____

NO6 **Model, represent and explain subtraction as comparison, take-away and part-to-whole.**

1. Which is a related subtraction fact that can be used to complete the number sentence?

$$6 + \boxed{} = 14$$

○ $8 - 6 = 2$

○ $14 - 10 = 4$

○ $14 - 6 = 8$

2. Haley has a bracelet with 12 beads. She gives 4 of the beads to her friend.

Which number sentence matches the problem?

○ $4 + 8 = 12$

○ $12 - 4 = 8$

○ $12 + 4 = 16$

3. Chandra had 5 marbles. Her sister gave her some more marbles. Now she has 12 marbles. Which number sentence shows how many marbles her sister gave her?

○ $12 - 5 = 7$

○ $12 - 7 = 4$

○ $12 + 5 = 17$

4. Sadie wrote this number sentence to solve a problem.

$$6 + \boxed{} = 15$$

What is the missing addend?

$$6 + \boxed{} = 15$$

$$15 - 6 = \boxed{}$$

○ 7

○ 8

○ 9

5. What is the missing addend?

$$\boxed{} + 9 = 12$$

$$12 - 9 = \boxed{}$$

○ 3

○ 4

○ 5

6. Jeff sees 3 grasshoppers. Tim sees 8 grasshoppers. How many fewer grasshoppers does Jeff see than Tim?

○ 4

○ 5

○ 6

7. Lila had 8 pencils. Ted gave her more. Now she has 13. How many pencils did Ted give Lila?

$$8 + \boxed{} = 13$$

$$13 - 8 = \boxed{}$$

○ 5

○ 7

○ 9

8. Maria and Rita go to the Mississippi River. Maria sees 11 catfish in the river. Rita sees 7 catfish. How many more catfish did Maria see than Rita?

Write the number sentence. Solve.

_____ ○ _____ ○ _____

_____ catfish

9. What is the missing addend?

$$\boxed{} + 9 = 17$$

$$17 - 9 = \boxed{}$$

The missing addend is _____.

10. Erin pours 8 glasses of lemonade for a picnic. We drink 4 of them right away. How many glasses of lemonade are left? Write a number sentence and solve.

_____ ○ _____ ○ _____

_____ glasses

Ohio Mathematics Achievement Test Practice

N07 **Model, represent and explain multiplication as repeated addition, rectangular arrays, and skip counting.**

1. Brit has 3 groups of 2 marbles. How many marbles does she have in all?

- ○ 2
- ○ 4
- ○ 6

2. Which multiplication sentence is shown?

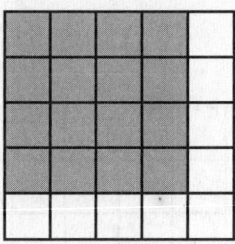

- ○ 2 × 8 = 16
- ○ 4 × 3 = 12
- ○ 4 × 4 = 16

3. Rick bought 5 trays with 3 red peppers in each tray. Which multiplication sentence shows how many peppers Rick has in all?

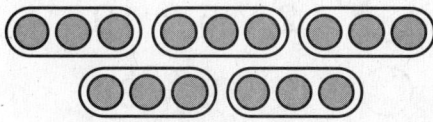

3 + 3 + 3 + 3 + 3 = ☐

- ○ 5 × 2 = 10
- ○ 5 × 3 = 15
- ○ 3 × 4 = 12

4. Shelby planted 4 rows of 5 strawberry plants. Which multiplication sentence shows how many she planted In all?

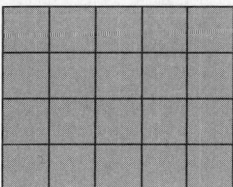

4 rows of 5

- ○ 4 × 5 = 20
- ○ 5 × 5 = 25
- ○ 3 × 5 = 15

5. **Which multiplication sentence shows how many counters in all?**

$2 + 2 + 2 + 2 =$ ☐

○ $2 \times 5 = 10$

○ $2 \times 4 = 8$

○ $4 \times 3 = 12$

6. **Lucy has 6 groups of 3 beads. Skip count. How many beads does Lucy have in all?**

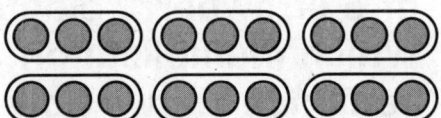

○ 12

○ 15

○ 18

7. **Write how many. Then write the multiplication sentence.**

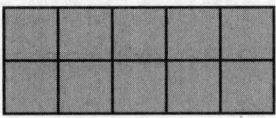

_____ rows of _____

___ ○ ___ ○ ___

8. **Color the array. Then complete the multiplication sentence.**

3 rows of 10

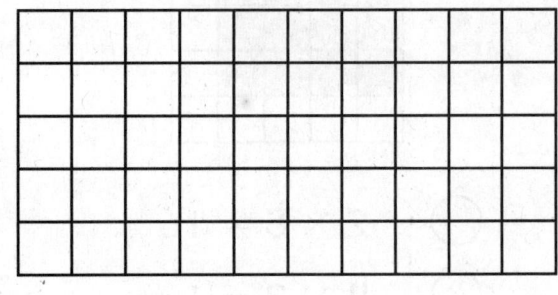

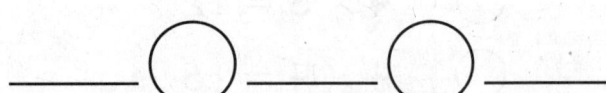

___ ○ ___ ○ ___

NO8 **Model, represent and explain division as sharing equally and repeated subtraction.**

1. Gianna has 10 muffins. She gives each friend 2 muffins. Which division sentence shows how many muffins each friend gets?

- ◯ $10 \div 2 = 5$
- ◯ $12 \div 2 = 6$
- ◯ $14 \div 2 = 7$

2. Jill has 12 books to give her sisters. She has 3 sisters. If each sister gets the same number of books, how many books does each sister get?

- ◯ 3
- ◯ 4
- ◯ 5

3. Amalia used the number line to divide 8 into equal groups of 4. What division sentence did she write?

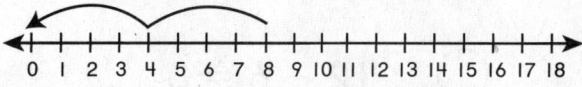

- ◯ $8 \div 1 = 8$
- ◯ $8 \div 4 = 2$
- ◯ $8 \div 2 = 10$

4. Which division sentence shows 16 ◯ divided into groups of 4?

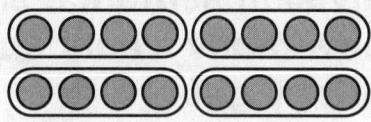

- ◯ $16 \div 4 = 2$
- ◯ $16 \div 4 = 3$
- ◯ $16 \div 4 = 4$

5. **Use the number line. Divide 12 into equal groups of 6.**

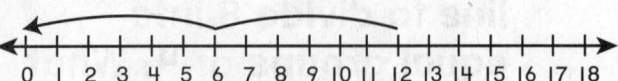

What is the division sentence?

○ $12 \div 6 = 3$

○ $12 \div 2 = 5$

○ $12 \div 2 = 6$

6. **Miguel has 14 treats to give to his puppies. There are 7 puppies. If each puppy gets the same number of treats, which division sentence shows how many treats each puppy gets?**

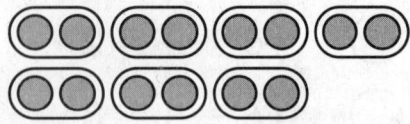

○ $14 \div 7 = 1$

○ $14 \div 7 = 2$

○ $14 \div 7 = 3$

7. **Draw ○ to divide 20 ○ into groups of 5. Write how many groups you draw.**

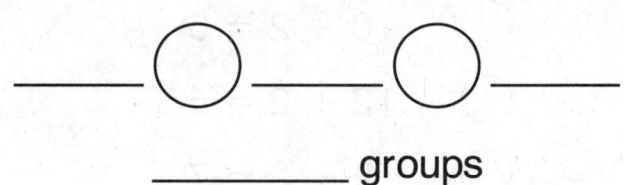

_____ groups

8. **Use the number line to write a division sentence.**

Divide 18 into equal groups of 6.

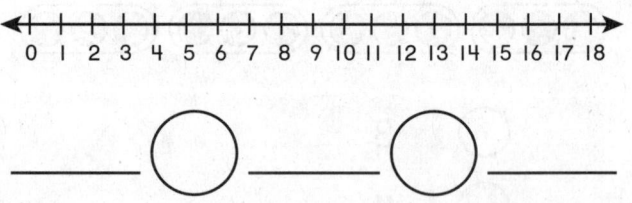

NO11 **Add and subtract multiples of 10.**

1. Count on tens to add. What is the sum?

$22 + 30 =$ ☐

- ◯ 32
- ◯ 42
- ◯ 52

2. Count back by tens to subtract. What is the difference?

$55 - 30 =$ ☐

- ◯ 25
- ◯ 35
- ◯ 45

3. Sadie has 17 ribbons. Then she buys 20 more ribbons. How many ribbons does she have now?

$17 + 20 =$ ☐

- ◯ 37 ribbons
- ◯ 47 ribbons
- ◯ 57 ribbons

4. What is the sum?

$36 + 40 =$ ☐

- ◯ 76
- ◯ 86
- ◯ 96

5. Samuel has 70 marbles. He gives 40 marbles away. How many marbles does Samuel have now?

$70 - 40 =$ ☐

- ◯ 20 marbles
- ◯ 30 marbles
- ◯ 40 marbles

6. What is the difference?

$64 - 40 =$ ☐

- ◯ 24
- ◯ 34
- ◯ 44

Standards Practice
93   Ohio Mathematics Achievement Test Practice

7. **Count on by tens to add. What is the sum?**

$$57 + 30 = \boxed{}$$

○ 67

○ 77

○ 87

8. **Count back ten to subtract. What is the difference?**

$$49 - 10 = \boxed{}$$

○ 29

○ 39

○ 49

9. **There are 81 birds on a fence. Then 50 birds fly away. How many birds are on the fence now?**

$$81 - 50 = \boxed{}$$

○ 21 birds

○ 31 birds

○ 41 birds

10. **Count on tens to add. Write the sum.**

$$28 + 20 = \boxed{}$$

11. **Matt has 72 crayons. He gives 30 crayons to his sister. How many crayons does he have now?**

_____ crayons

12. **Write the sum.**

$$41 + 50 = \boxed{}$$

13. **There are 24 children on a bus. Then 40 more children join them. How many children are on the bus now?**

_____ children

14. **Count back by tens to subtract. Write the difference.**

$$92 - 20 = \boxed{}$$

NO12 Demonstrate multiple strategies for adding and subtracting 2- or 3-digit whole numbers.

1. **What is the difference?**

Workmat

Tens	Ones

Tens	Ones
3	0
−	4

- ○ 25
- ○ 26
- ○ 34

2. **What is the difference?**

Hundreds	Tens	Ones
4	5	4
− 2	3	8

- ○ 214
- ○ 216
- ○ 226

3. There are 14 ladybugs on a leaf. There are 17 ladybugs on a branch. How many ladybugs are there in all?

- ○ 21 ladybugs
- ○ 23 ladybugs
- ○ 31 ladybugs

4. Mark brings 15 sandwiches for a camping trip. Stacy brings 18 sandwiches. How many sandwiches do Mark and Stacy bring in all?

Tens	Ones
1	5
+ 1	8

- ○ 22 sandwiches
- ○ 23 sandwiches
- ○ 33 sandwiches

5. **What is the sum?**

Workmat

Tens	Ones

Tens	Ones
☐	☐
3	9
3	7

+

○ 66

○ 67

○ 76

6. **What is the difference?**

Workmat

Tens	Ones

Tens	Ones
☐	☐
2	7
1	9

−

○ 8

○ 11

○ 18

7. **Subtract. Then add to check.**

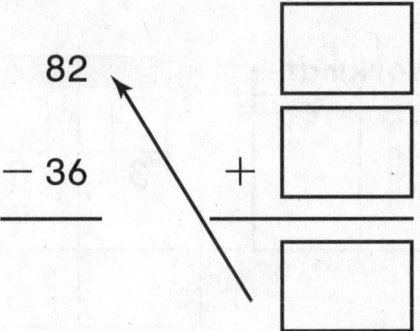

82

− 36

+

8. **What is the sum?**

Hundreds	Tens	Ones
☐	☐	☐
4	6	3
3	5	2

+

9. **Rita has 864 coins. Henry has 514 coins. How many more coins does Rita have then Henry?**

Hundreds	Tens	Ones
☐	☐	☐
8	6	4
5	1	4

−

_____ more coins

Name _____

NO13 Estimate the results of whole number addition and subtraction problems using front-end estimation, and judge the reasonableness of the answers.

1. Round each number to the nearest hundred. What is the estimated difference?

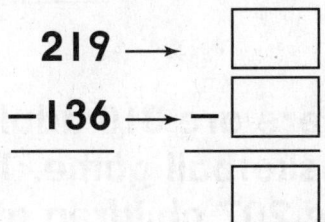

219 → ☐
−136 → − ☐
            ☐

○ 100
○ 200
○ 300

2. Round each addend to the nearest ten. What is the estimated sum?

32 → ☐
+51 → + ☐
          ☐

○ 70
○ 80
○ 90

3. Round each number to the nearest hundred. What is the estimated sum?

122 → ☐
+216 → + ☐
             ☐

○ 100
○ 200
○ 300

4. Amanda has 32 socks in her drawer. Her brother has 24 socks in his drawer. About how many more socks does Amanda have than her brother?

○ about 10 more socks
○ about 20 more socks
○ about 30 more socks

5. **Round each number to the nearest ten. What is the estimated sum?**

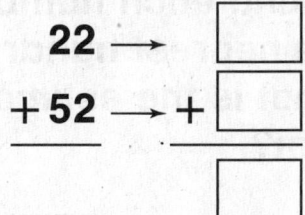

$$22 \rightarrow \boxed{}$$
$$+52 \rightarrow +\boxed{}$$
$$\boxed{}$$

◯ 50

◯ 60

◯ 70

6. **Round each number to the nearest hundred. What is the estimated difference?**

$$621 \rightarrow \boxed{}$$
$$-517 \rightarrow -\boxed{}$$
$$\boxed{}$$

◯ 100

◯ 200

◯ 300

7. **Round each number to the nearest ten. Write the estimated difference.**

$$63 \rightarrow \boxed{}$$
$$-54 \rightarrow -\boxed{}$$
$$\boxed{}$$

8. **There are 310 adults at a basketball game. There are 207 children at the basketball game. About how many people are at the basketball game in all?**

$$310 \rightarrow \boxed{}$$
$$+207 \rightarrow +\boxed{}$$
$$\boxed{}$$

about _____ people

9. **Paula and Eric play a game. Paula has 419 points. Eric has 224 points. Round each score to the nearest hundred. About how many more points does Paula have then Eric?**

about _____ more points

MI **Identify and select appropriate units of measure for: a. length – centimeters, meters, inches, feet, or yards; b. volume (capacity) – liters, cups, pints, or quarts; c. weight – grams, ounces, or pounds; d time – hours, half hours, quarter-hours or minutes and time designations, a.m. or p.m.**

1. **Which unit is best to measure the mass of a computer?**

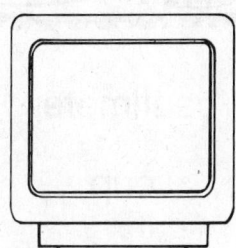

○ kilogram

○ gram

○ liter

2. **At which time is a child most likely to come home from school?**

○ 3:00 a.m.

○ 5:00 a.m.

○ 3:00 p.m.

3. **Jerome has a small thermos of soup. Which unit is best to measure the capacity of Jerome's thermos?**

○ quart

○ cup

○ gallon

4. **Which unit is best to measure the length of the crayon?**

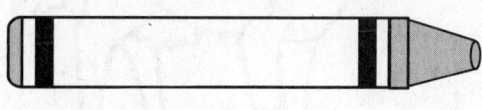

○ inch

○ foot

○ yard

5. **About how long will it take to play a game of kickball?**

- ○ about 1 hour
- ○ about 8 hours
- ○ about 2 minutes

6. **Which unit is best to measure the weight of a cow?**

- ○ ounce
- ○ pound
- ○ meter

7. **Frank wants to measure the length of his shoe. Circle the best unit to measure the length of Frank's shoe.**

centimeter

cup

meter

8. **Sammy has a pitcher of water. Circle the best unit to measure the capacity Sammy's pitcher.**

quart

cup

pint

M2 **Establish personal or common referents for units of measure to make estimates and comparisons; e.g. the width of a finger is a centimeter, a large bottle of soda pop is 2 liters, a small paper clip weighs about one gram.**

1. **Danny has a pen. Which shows the best estimate for the weight of Danny's pen?**

   ○ about 4 ounces

   ○ about 4 pounds

   ○ about 40 pounds

2. **Marcy has a pencil. Which shows the best estimate for the length of Marcy's pencil?**

   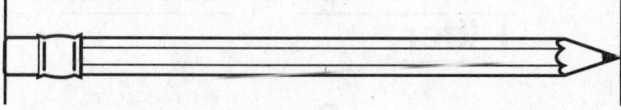

   ○ about 8 meters

   ○ about 80 centimeters

   ○ about 8 centimeters

3. **Morgan has a paper clip. Which shows the best estimate for the mass of Morgan's paper clip?**

   ○ about 1 kilogram

   ○ about 1 gram

   ○ about 100 grams

4. **Meghan has a ribbon. About how long is Meghan's ribbon?**

   ○ about 2 inches

   ○ about 2 feet

   ○ about 2 yards

5. **About how long is the fence?**

- ◯ about 10 centimeters
- ◯ about 50 centimeters
- ◯ about 10 meters

6. **Which has a mass of about 1 kilogram?**

◯

◯

◯

7. **Circle the best estimate for the height of a woman.**

about 5 inches

about 5 feet

about 5 yards

8. **Julie has a mug. About how much can Julie's mug hold? Circle more than 1 liter or less than 1 liter.**

more than 1 liter

less than 1 liter

M3 **Describe and compare the relationships among units of measure.**

M7 **Make and test predictions about measurements, using different units to measure the same length or volume.**

1. **Allison read a book for 1 hour. Which amount of time is the same as 1 hour?**

- ○ 7 days
- ○ 60 minutes
- ○ 52 weeks

2. **The milk container holds 1 gallon. How many cups does the container hold?**

- ○ 2 cups
- ○ 4 cups
- ○ 16 cups

3. **Wendy measures the length of a stick. It is 1 foot long. How many inches long is the stick?**

- ○ 6 inches
- ○ 12 inches
- ○ 18 inches

4. **The bulletin board is 1 meter long. How many centimeters long is the bulletin board?**

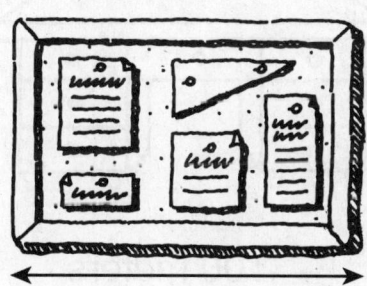

- ○ 1 centimeter
- ○ 10 centimeters
- ○ 100 centimeters

5. The container holds I pint. How many cups does the container hold?

ICE CREAM

○ 2 cups

○ 4 cups

○ 16 cups

6. The teacher's desk is 100 centimeters long. How many meters long is the teacher's desk?

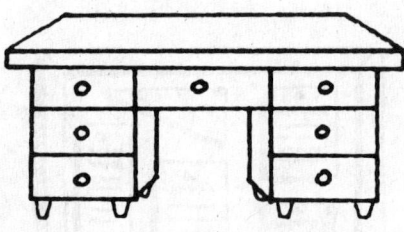

○ 100 meters

○ 10 meters

○ 1 meter

7. Ryan's puppy is 7 months old. Write more than, less than, or the same as to complete the sentence.

This is _____ I year.

8. About how much might the swimming pool hold? Circle more than I liter or less than I liter.

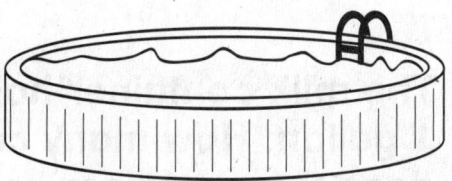

more than I liter

less than I liter

M4 Tell time to the nearest minute interval on digital and to the nearest 5 minute interval on analog (dial) timepieces.

1. Which clock shows twenty minutes before twelve?

2. What time does the clock show?

○ 1:55

○ 2:11

○ 2:55

3. Which clock shows 9:05?

4. What time does the clock show?

○ 2:45

○ 3:45

○ 9:10

5. **Which shows another way to write the time?**

○ 10 minutes before 6

○ 10 minutes before 7

○ 50 minutes before 8

7. **Draw the minute hand to show the time.**

6. **Which clock shows the same time?**

○ 1:20

○ 1:30

○ 6:05

8. **Write the time in another way.**

_____ minutes after

_____ o'clock

M5 **Estimate and measure the length and weight of common objects, using metric and U.S. customary units, accurate to the nearest unit.**

1. **Which shows the best estimate for the mass of a baseball bat?**

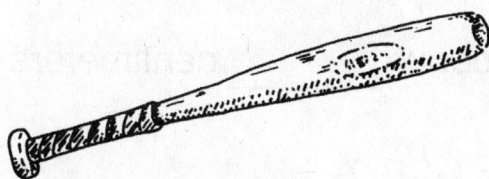

- ⃝ about 1 gram
- ⃝ about 10 grams
- ⃝ about 1 kilogram

2. **Use a centimeter ruler. What is the length of the string to the nearest centimeter?**

- ⃝ about 2 centimeters
- ⃝ about 4 centimeters
- ⃝ about 6 centimeters

3. **Which shows the best estimate for the mass of a crayon?**

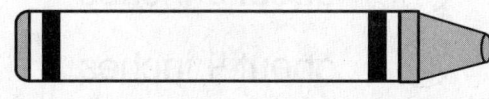

- ⃝ about 20 grams
- ⃝ about 2 kilograms
- ⃝ about 20 kilograms

4. **Which shows the best estimate for the weight of a peach?**

- ⃝ about 4 ounces
- ⃝ about 4 pounds
- ⃝ about 40 ounces

Name _____

5. Use an inch ruler. What is the length to the nearest inch?

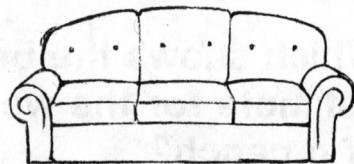

- ○ about 3 inches
- ○ about 4 inches
- ○ about 5 inches

6. About how long is a sofa?

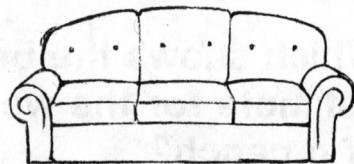

- ○ about 2 centimeters
- ○ about 2 meters
- ○ about 20 meters

7. About how much do the grapes weigh?

- ○ about 40 ounces
- ○ about 4 pounds
- ○ about 4 ounces

8. Use a centimeter ruler. Measure the length of the crayon to the nearest centimeter.

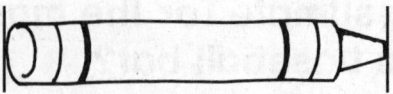

about _____ centimeters

9. Use an inch ruler. Measure the length of the ribbon to the nearest inch.

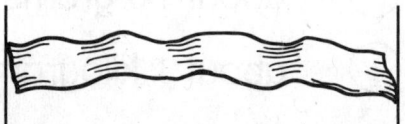

about _____ inches

10. Circle the object that has a mass of about 5 grams.

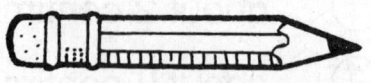

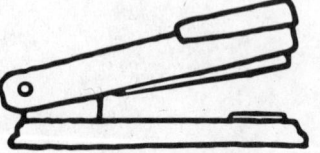

M6 **Select and use appropriate measurement tools; e.g., a ruler to draw a segment 3 inches long, a measuring cup to place 2 cups of rice in a bowl, a scale to weigh 50 grams of candy.**

1. **Darla wants to find out how many centimeters long her paper is. Which measuring tool should Darla use?**

    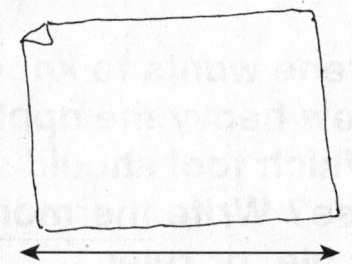

    ○ a centimeter ruler

    ○ an inch ruler

    ○ a cup

2. **Elliot is measuring the weight of an orange. Which measuring tool should Elliot use?**

    ○ a cup

    ○ an inch ruler

    ○ a scale

3. **Use a ruler. About how long is the chalk?**

    ○ about 4 centimeters

    ○ about 40 centimeters

    ○ about 4 meters

4. **Devin wants to find out how hot his soup is. Which tool should he use?**

    ○ a scale

    ○ a measuring cup

    ○ a thermometer

5. **Xavier wants to cut a piece of yarn that is 15 inches long. Which tool should he use?**

- ○ a centimeter ruler
- ○ a scale
- ○ an inch ruler

6. **Olivia wants to put 10 gallons of water into her fish tank. Which container should she use?**

○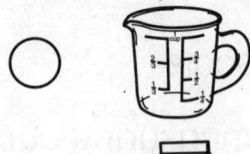

○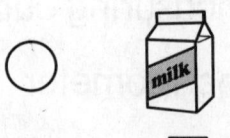

○

7. **What is the length of the string to the nearest inch?**

_____ inches

8. **Irene wants to know how heavy the apple is. Which tool should she use? Write thermometer, scale, or ruler.**

_____

9. **What is the length of the stick to the nearest centimeter?**

_____ centimeters

Standards Practice

110   Ohio Mathematics Achievement Test Practice

GI **Identify, describe, compare, and sort three-dimensional objects (i.e., cubes, spheres, prisms, cones, cylinders, and pyramids) according to the shape of the faces or the number of faces, edges, or vertices.**

1. **Which figure has 6 faces, 12 edges, and 8 vertices?**

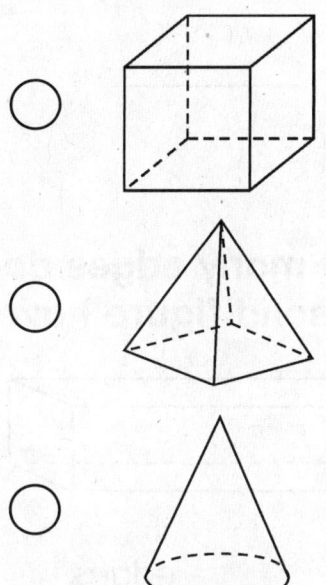

2. **Which solid figure can slide and roll?**

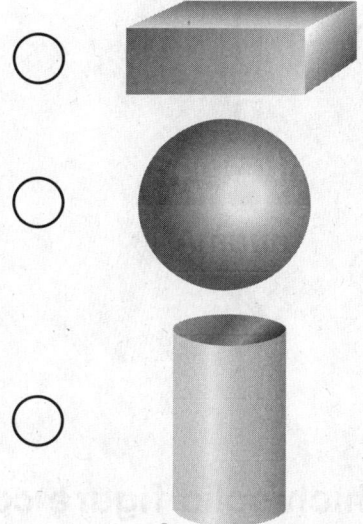

2. **Which solid figure has these faces?**

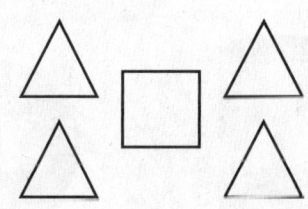

○ cylinder
○ pyramid
○ cube

4. **How many vertices does the solid figure have?**

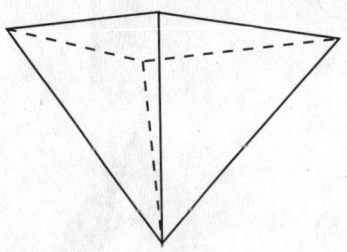

○ 5 vertices
○ 6 vertices
○ 8 vertices

5. **Which solid figure has 6 faces?**

○
○
○

6. **Which solid figure can slide, but cannot roll?**

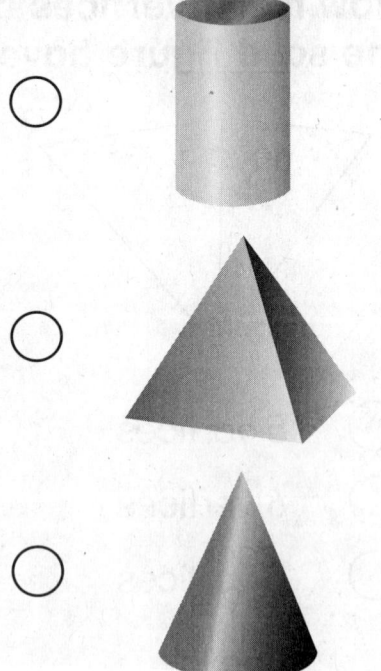

○
○
○

7. **Write the name of the solid figure.**

_____

8. **How many edges does the solid figure have?**

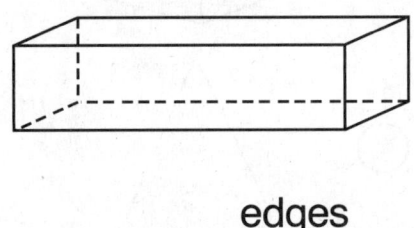

_____ edges

9. **Circle the sphere.**

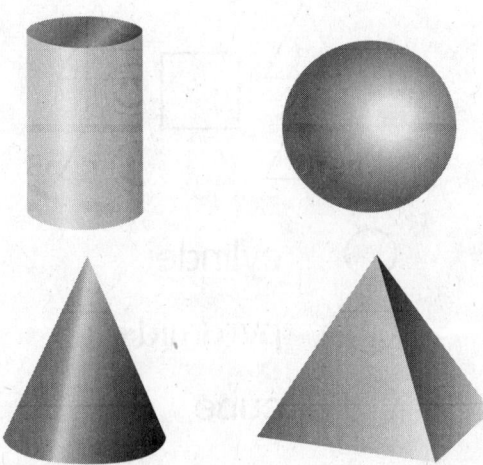

G2 **Predict what new shapes will be formed by combining or cutting apart existing shapes.**

1. Cindy cuts the paper shape along the dotted line.

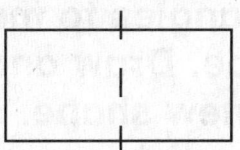

Which new shapes does Cindy make?

○ 2 squares

○ 2 pentagons

○ 2 hexagons

2. Dario has 2 shapes.

He combines the 2 shapes. Which new shape might Dario make?

○

○

○

3. Rob cuts the paper figure on the dotted line.

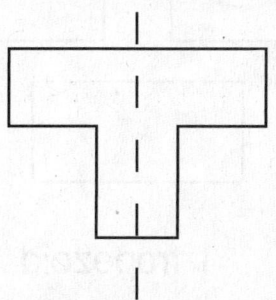

Which new figures does Rob make?

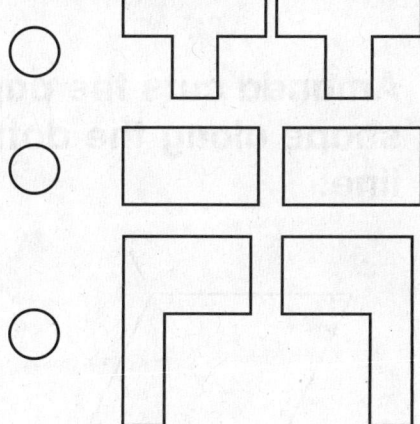

○

○

○

4. Which figure can you make if you combine 2 squares?

○ 1 triangle

○ 1 rectangle

○ 1 pentagon

5. **Which figure can you make if you combine 3 rectangles?**

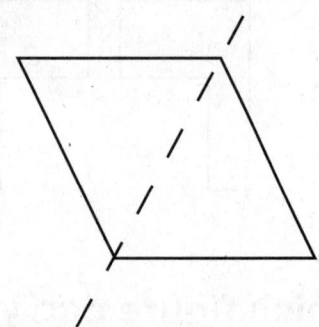

- ○ I trapezoid
- ○ I rectangle
- ○ I triangle

6. **Amanda cuts the paper shape along the dotted line.**

Which new shapes does Amanda make?

- ○ 2 triangles
- ○ 2 squares
- ○ 2 trapezoids

7. **Brian has 3 triangles.**

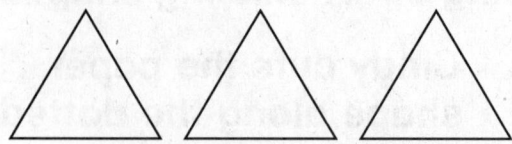

He combines the 3 triangles to make a new shape. Draw and name the new shape.

_____

8. **Eve has 5 triangles.**

She combines the 5 triangles to make a new shape. Draw and name the new shape.

G3 Recognize two-dimensional shapes and three-dimensional objects from different positions.

1. Julie has a plane figure. It has more than 3 sides. Each side is the same length. Which figure might Julie have?

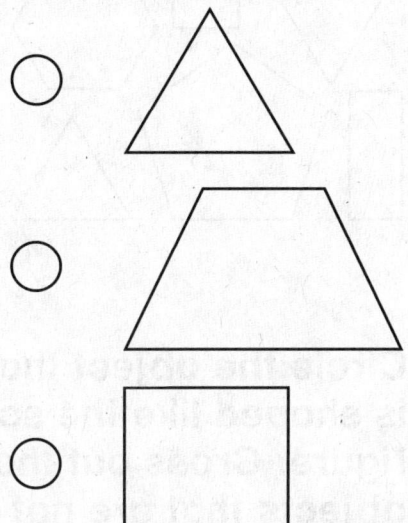

○

○

○

2. Which title is best for the group of plane figures?

○ figures with 4 sides

○ figures with 3 sides

○ figures with 5 sides

3. Which solid figure has some faces that are triangles?

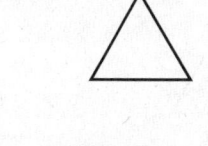

○ cone

○ pyramid

○ cylinder

4. Which object is shaped like a sphere?

○

○

○

5. **How has the figure moved?**

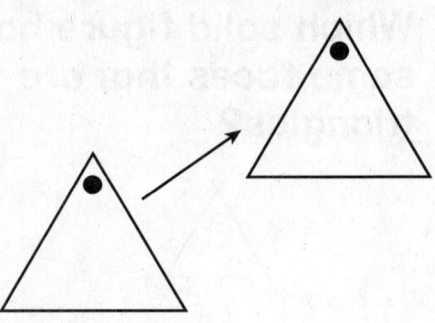

- ◯ slide
- ◯ flip
- ◯ turn

6. **Which solid figure has these faces?**

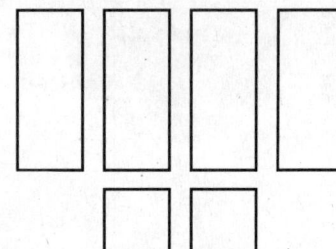

- ◯ cube
- ◯ pyramid
- ◯ rectangular prism

7. **Mandy wants to make a group of figures with more than 3 vertices. Cross out the figures that do not belong in Mandy's group.**

8. **Circle the object that is shaped like the solid figure. Cross out the objects that are not shaped like the solid figure.**

G4 **Identify and determine whether two-dimensional shapes are congruent (same shape and size) or similar (same shape different size) by copying or using superposition (lay one thing on top of another).**

1. **Which shows similar figures?**

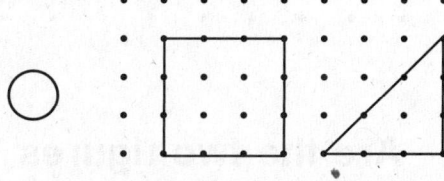

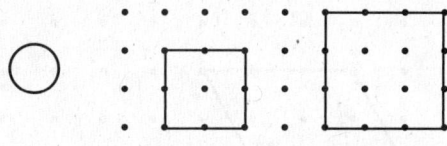

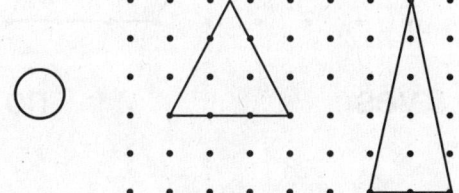

2. **Which sentence is true about congruent figures?**

    ◯ They have different shapes.

    ◯ They have different sizes.

    ◯ They have the same size and same shape.

3. **Which figure is congruent to the triangle?**

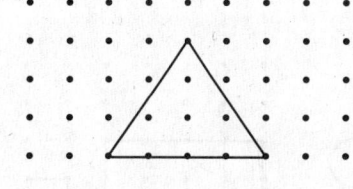

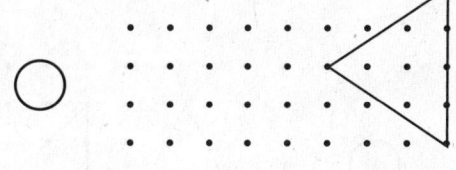

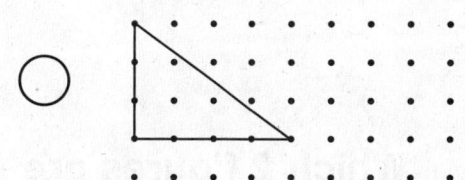

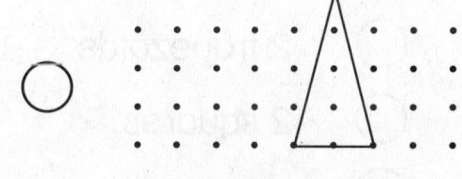

4. Which shows similar figures?

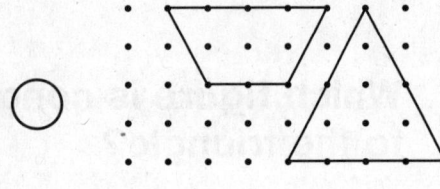

5. Which 2 figures are always similar?

○ 2 trapezoids

○ 2 squares

○ 2 triangles

6. Draw a figure congruent to the figure shown.

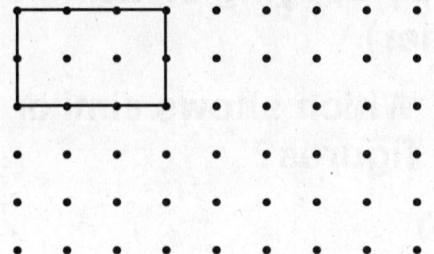

7. Are the two figures congruent? Circle <u>yes</u> or <u>no</u>.

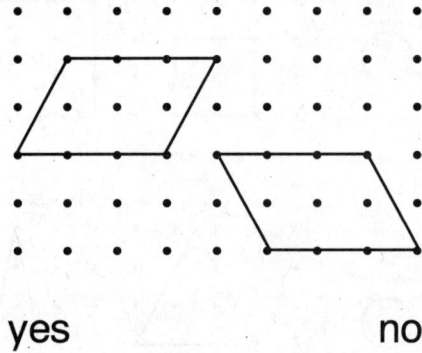

yes   no

8. Draw a figure congruent to the figure shown.

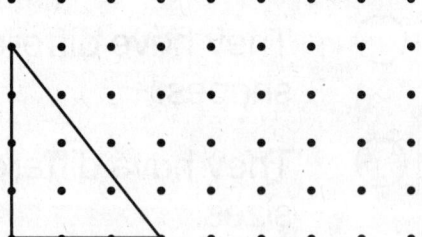

G5 **Create and identify two-dimensional figures with line symmetry; e.g., what letter shapes, logos, polygons are symmetrical?**

1. **Which shows a line of symmetry?**

   ○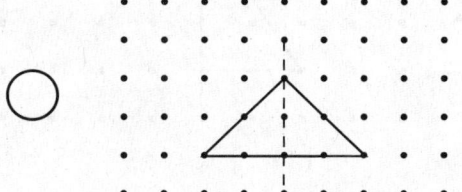

   ○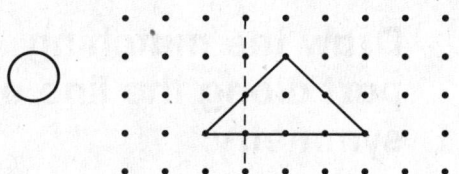

   ○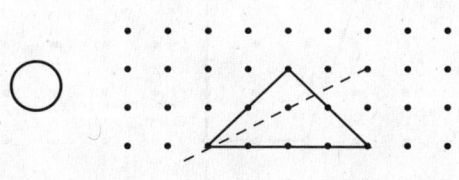

3. **Which shows a line of symmetry?**

   ○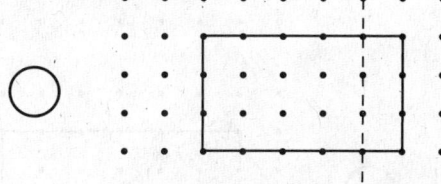

   ○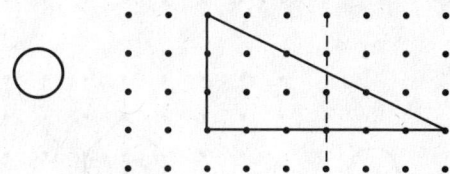

   ○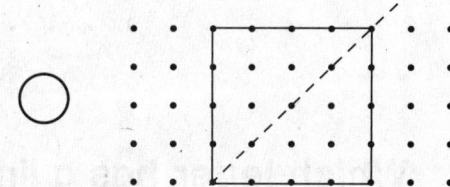

2. **Which letter has a line of symmetry?**

   ○ O
   ○ P
   ○ R

4. **Which letter has a line of symmetry?**

   ○ A
   ○ G
   ○ Z

5. **Which shows a line of symmetry?**

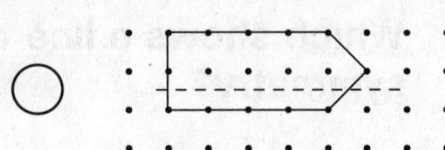

○

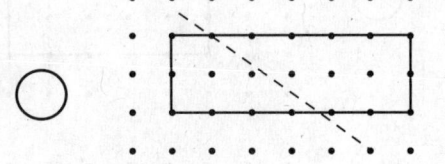

○

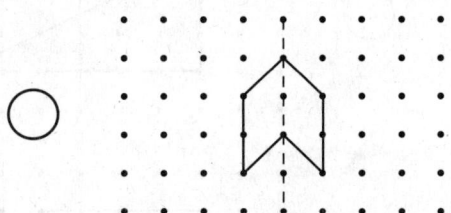

○

6. **Which letter has a line of symmetry?**

○ T

○ F

○ J

7. **Draw the matching part along the line of symmetry.**

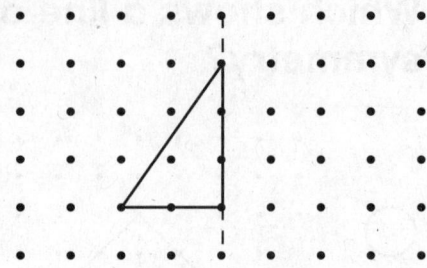

8. **Draw the matching part along the line of symmetry.**

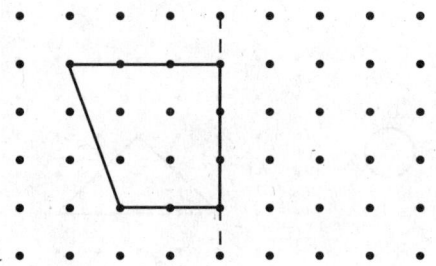

9. **Circle the figures that show a line of symmetry.**

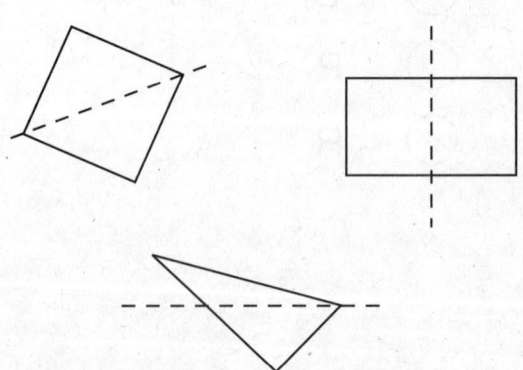

AI Extend simple number patterns (both repeating and growing patterns), and create similar patterns using different objects, such as using physical materials or shapes to represent numerical patterns.

1. Which shows the pattern unit?

○

○

○

2. Which number comes next in the repeating pattern?

38, 5, 51, 38, 5, 51, 38, 5, _____

○ 5

○ 38

○ 51

3. Which shows the next two figures in the pattern?

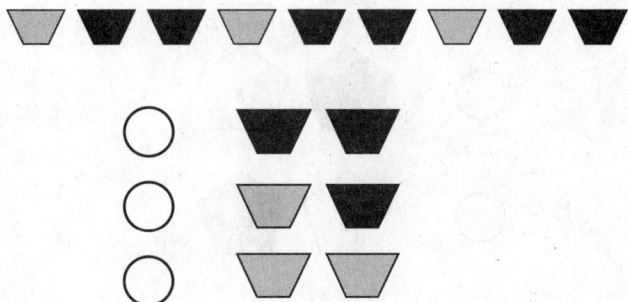

○

○

○

4. Use the hundred chart. Skip-count by fives. Which numbers come next?

1	2	3	4	5	6	7	8	9	10
11	12	13	14	15	16	17	18	19	20
21	22	23	24	25	26	27	28	29	30
31	32	33	34	35	36	37	38	39	40
41	42	43	44	45	46	47	48	49	50
51	52	53	54	55	56	57	58	59	60
61	62	63	64	65	66	67	68	69	70

21, 26, 31, _____, _____

○ 41, 51

○ 38, 43

○ 36, 41

5. Which shows the next two figures of the pattern?

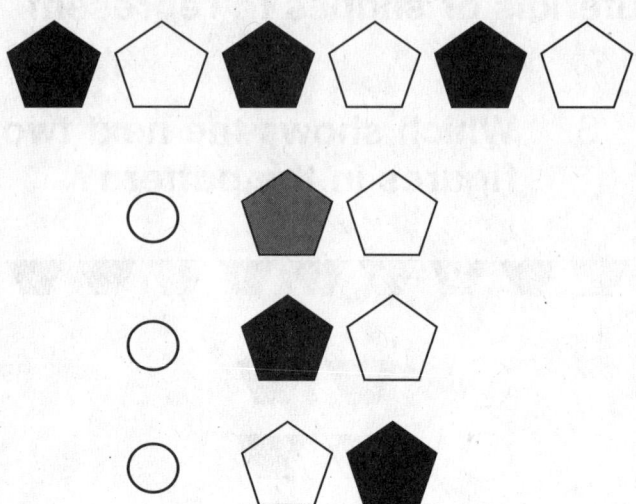

- ○   (gray pentagon) (white pentagon)
- ○   (black pentagon) (white pentagon)
- ○   (white pentagon) (black pentagon)

6. Which pattern does the hundred chart show?

1	2	3	4	5	6	7	8	9	10
11	12	13	14	15	16	17	18	19	20
21	22	23	24	25	26	27	28	29	30
31	32	33	34	35	36	37	38	39	40
41	42	43	44	45	46	47	48	49	50
51	52	53	54	55	56	57	58	59	60
61	62	63	64	65	66	67	68	69	70
71	72	73	74	75	76	77	78	79	80
81	82	83	84	85	86	87	88	89	90
91	92	93	94	95	96	97	98	99	100

- ○   Count by twos.
- ○   Count by threes.
- ○   Count by fives.

7. Draw the missing piece of the pattern.

↑ • ↑ • • ↑ • • ↑ ___ •

8. Write a rule for the pattern. Then extend the pattern.

Rule: Count by _____.

245, 250, 255, 260, _____, _____

9. Skip count by fives. Show the pattern on the hundred chart. Circle the numbers.

1	2	3	4	5	6	7	8	9	10
11	12	13	14	15	16	17	18	19	20
21	22	23	24	25	26	27	28	29	30
31	32	33	34	35	36	37	38	39	40
41	42	43	44	45	46	47	48	49	50
51	52	53	54	55	56	57	58	59	60
61	62	63	64	65	66	67	68	69	70
71	72	73	74	75	76	77	78	79	80
81	82	83	84	85	86	87	88	89	90
91	92	93	94	95	96	97	98	99	100

Name ______________________________ **Standards Practice**

A2 Use patterns to make generalization and predictions; e.g., determine a missing element in a pattern.

1. **What are the next two shapes in the pattern?**

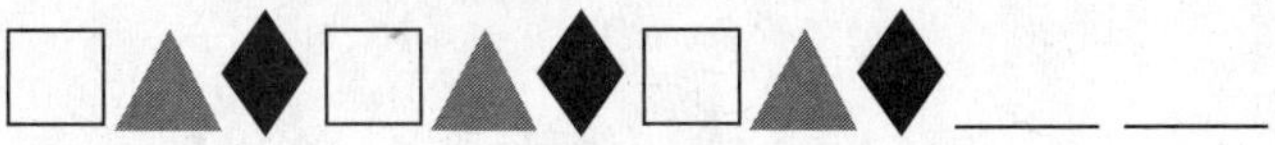

○ 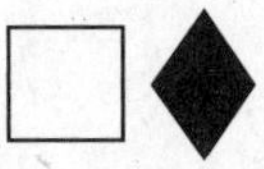

○ 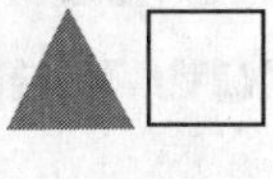

○ 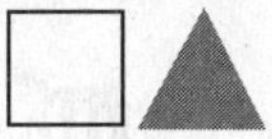

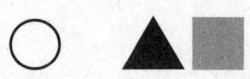

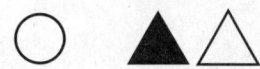

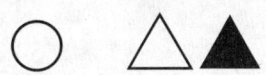

2. **What is the missing piece in the pattern?**

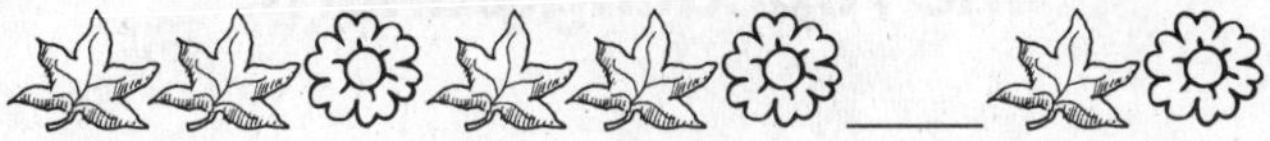

○ 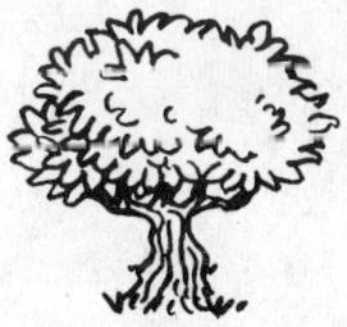

○ 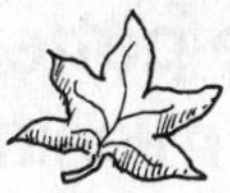

○ 

3. **What are the next two shapes in the pattern?**

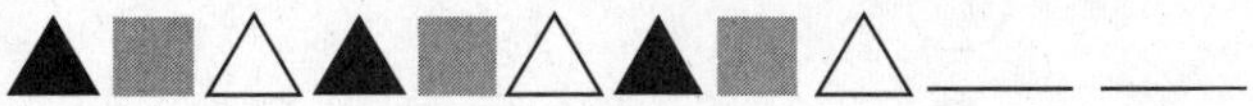

○ 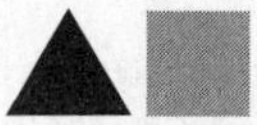

○ 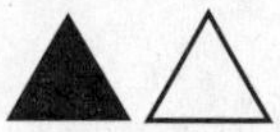

○ 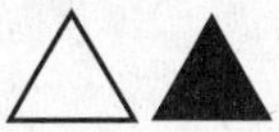

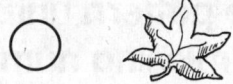

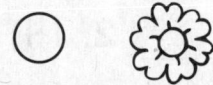

4. **What is the missing piece in the pattern?**

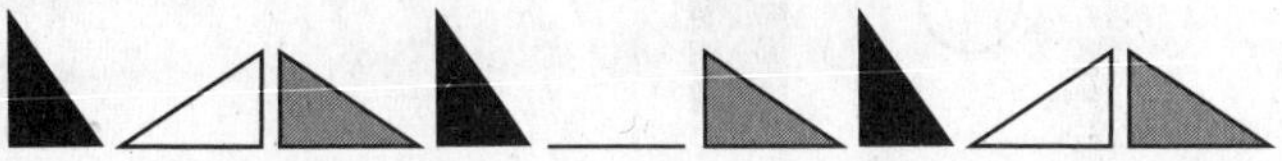

○ 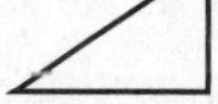

○ 

○ 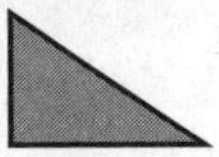

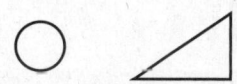

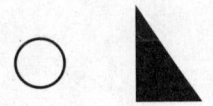

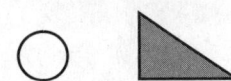

Name _____

5. What number is missing in the repeating pattern?

5, 1, 7, 5, 1, 7 _____, 1, 7

○ 1

○ 5

○ 7

6. What is the missing piece in the pattern?

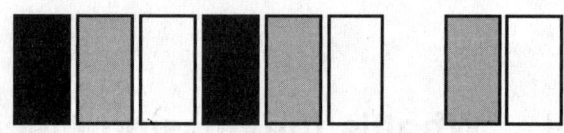

○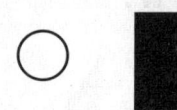

○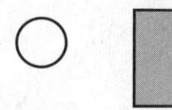

○

7. Circle the pattern unit. Then draw the missing piece.

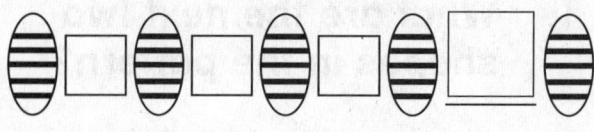

8. Circle the pattern unit. Then draw what comes next.

9. Circle the pattern unit. Then write the missing number in the repeating pattern.

1, 9, 18, 1, 9, 18, _____, 9, 18

10. Circle the pattern unit. Then write the missing number in the repeating pattern.

14, 7, 2, 14, _____, 2, 14, 7, 2

A3 Create new patterns with consistent rules or plans, and describe the rule or general plan of existing patterns.

1. Look at the number line. Which shows the rule for the pattern?

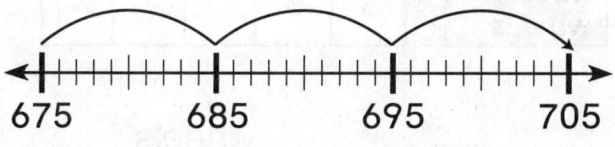

675   685   695   705

○ Count by tens.

○ Count by fives.

○ Count by twos.

2. Dana has some CDs. There are 10 songs on each CD. How many songs are on 5 CDs? Complete the table to solve.

number of CDs	1	2	3	4	5
number of songs	10	20	30		

○ 35 songs

○ 40 songs

○ 50 songs

3. What is the rule for the table?

In	Out
2	4
3	5
4	6
5	7

○ Add 4.

○ Add 3.

○ Add 2.

4. Carlos gets 2 magazines each month in the mail. How many magazines does he get in 5 months? Complete the table to solve.

number of months	1	2	3	4	5
number of magazines	2	4			

○ 8 magazines

○ 10 magazines

○ 12 magazines

Ohio Mathematics Achievement Test Practice

5. **What number is missing from the table?**

Rule: Add 5.

In	Out
0	5
2	7
4	
6	11

○ 9

○ 10

○ 11

6. **Skip count by tens. What are the next two numbers?**

355, 365, 375, ___, ___

○ 385, 390

○ 385, 395

○ 395, 400

7. **There are 3 wheels on 1 tricycle. How many wheels are on 5 tricycles?**

number of tricycles	1	2	3	4	5
number of wheels	3	6			

_____ wheels

8. **Alicia writes 4 pages in her journal each week. How many pages does Alicia write in 5 weeks?**

number of weeks	1	2	3	4	5
number of pages	4	8			

_____ pages

9. **Write the rule. Then complete the table.**

Rule: Add _____.

In	Out
1	5
2	6
3	
4	

A4 **Use objects, pictures, numbers and other symbols to represent a problem situation.**

1. There are 4 bowls. There are 5 grapes in each bowl. Which number sentence tells how many grapes there are in all?

   ○ $4 \times 5 = 20$

   ○ $5 - 4 = 1$

   ○ $4 + 5 = 9$

2. Gina and her friends have marbles. They make the table below to show how many marbles each child has.

Our Marbles	
Name	Number of Marbles
Gina	35
Max	46
Dan	29
Rita	38

   How many marbles do Gina and Dan have in all?

   ○ 148 marbles

   ○ 81 marbles

   ○ 64 marbles

3. There are 67 markers and 24 crayons. How many markers and crayons are there in all?

   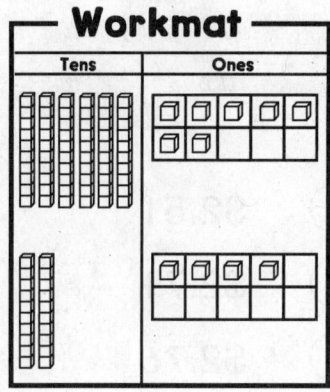

   ○ 91

   ○ 81

   ○ 71

4. How many squares do you need to make 4 cubes?

number of cubes	1	2	3	4
number of squares	6	12	18	

   ○ 12 squares

   ○ 18 squares

   ○ 24 squares

Ohio Mathematics Achievement Test Practice

5. Tina has 2 dollars, 2 quarters, 2 dimes, and 1 penny. How much money does she have?

- ○ $2.51
- ○ $2.71
- ○ $2.76

6. The teacher gives 3 pens to each child. How many pens does the teacher give to 5 children?

number of children	1	2	3	4	5
number of pens	3	6	9	12	

- ○ 5
- ○ 15
- ○ 16

7. Wendy has 1 quarter, 2 dimes, 1 nickel, and 2 pennies.

Does she have enough money to buy the banana? Write yes or no.

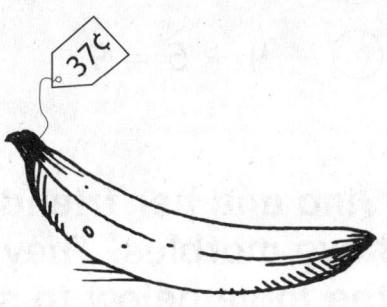

_____

8. Jim has 11 baseball cards. He gives 4 of the baseball cards to his friends. How many baseball cards does Jim have left? Write a number sentence and solve.

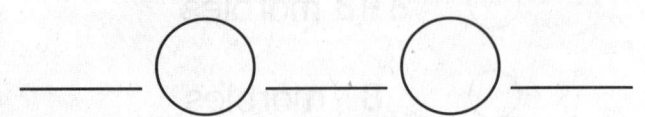

_____ baseball cards

A5 **Understand equivalence and extend the concept to situations involving symbols; e.g., $4 + 5 = 9$ and $5 + 4 = 9$, and $4 + 5 = 3 + 6 = \triangle + \square$.**

1. **What number will complete the number sentence?**

$$8 - \square = 2 + 4$$

- ◯ 1
- ◯ 2
- ◯ 3

2. **Which number is missing in both boxes?**

Since $5 + \square = 11$,

then $11 - 5 = \square$.

- ◯ 6
- ◯ 4
- ◯ 3

3. **What number will complete the number sentence?**

$$3 + 5 = \square + 4$$

- ◯ 2
- ◯ 3
- ◯ 4

4. **What number will complete the number sentence?**

$$\square + 5 = 6 + 6$$

- ◯ 6
- ◯ 7
- ◯ 8

5. **Elijah has 7 blue crayons and 8 red crayons. Jana has 9 blue crayons and some red crayons. Elijah and Jana have the same number of crayons. How many red crayons does Jana have?**

$$7 + 8 = 9 + \square$$

- ◯ 5 red crayons
- ◯ 6 red crayons
- ◯ 7 red crayons

6. **What number will complete the number sentence?**

$$18 - \boxed{} = 15 - 1$$

- ○ 4
- ○ 3
- ○ 2

7. **What number will complete the number sentence?**

$$5 + 2 = \boxed{} - 3$$

- ○ 7
- ○ 8
- ○ 10

8. **What number will complete the number sentence?**

$$6 + 7 = 10 + \boxed{}$$

- ○ 3
- ○ 4
- ○ 5

9. **Write the number that will complete the number sentence.**

$$12 - \boxed{} = 10 - 1$$

10. **Write the number that will complete the number sentence.**

$$9 - 4 = 6 - \boxed{}$$

11. **John has 6 pennies and some nickels. Mike has 8 pennies and 7 nickels. Each child has the same number of coins in all. How many nickels does John have?**

$$6 + \boxed{} = 8 + 7$$

_____ nickles

12. **Write the number that will complete the number sentence.**

$$2 + \boxed{} = 12 - 4$$

A6 Use symbols to represent unknown quantities and identify values for symbols in an expression or equation using addition and subtraction; e.g., $\square + \bigcirc = 10$, $\triangle - 2 = 4$.

1. What is the missing addend?

    $6 + \square = 14$

    ○ 7
    ○ 8
    ○ 20

2. What number is missing from both boxes?

    Since $7 + \square = 11$,

    then $11 - 7 = \square$.

    ○ 3
    ○ 4
    ○ 6

3. What is the missing addend?

    $5 + \square = 13$

    ○ 4
    ○ 6
    ○ 8

4. What is the missing number?

    $\square - 5 = 3$

    ○ 2
    ○ 8
    ○ 9

5. What number does $\triangle$ stand for?

    $6 + \triangle = 10$

    ○ 4
    ○ 5
    ○ 16

6. Meena had 11 stickers. She gave some to her sister. Now Meena has 6 stickers. How many stickers did Meena give her sister?

    $11 - \square = 6$

    ○ 2 stickers
    ○ 5 stickers
    ○ 17 stickers

7. **What number is missing from both boxes?**

   Since $9 + \boxed{} = 15$,

   then $15 - 9 = \boxed{}$.

   ○ 3

   ○ 6

   ○ 12

8. **What is the missing addend?**

   $8 + \boxed{} = 15$

   ○ 7

   ○ 9

   ○ 11

9. **What number does the △ stand for?**

   $14 = 6 + \triangle$

   ○ 6

   ○ 7

   ○ 8

10. **Complete both number sentences.**

    $4 + \boxed{} = 13$

    $13 - 4 = \boxed{}$

11. **What number does the △ stand for?**

    $12 - \triangle = 5$

    $\triangle = \underline{}$

12. **Complete both number sentences.**

    $\boxed{} + 2 = 10$

    $10 - 2 = \boxed{}$

13. **What number does the ☆ stand for?**

    $☆ + 4 = 8$

    $☆ = \underline{}$

A7 Describe qualitative and quantitative changes, especially those involving addition and subtraction; e.g., a student growing taller versus a student growing two inches in one year.

1. **How did Joe's height change from age 1 to age 5?**

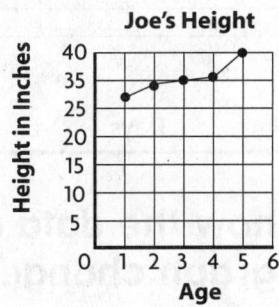

Joe's Height

○ He grew shorter.

○ He grew 20 inches.

○ He grew taller.

2. **How much more snow fell in March than in December?**

Snowfall in Winterville	
Month	**Amount of Snow**
December	1 inch
January	7 inches
February	5 inches
March	3 inches

○ 2 inches

○ 7 inches

○ 8 inches

3. **How did the number of children change from 3:00 to 6:00?**

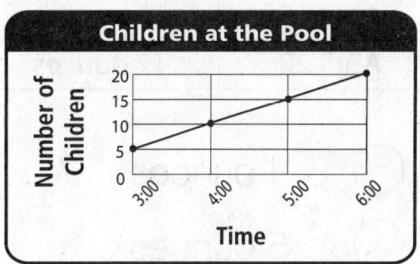

Children at the Pool

○ There were fewer children at 6:00.

○ There were more children at 3:00.

○ There were more children at 6:00.

4. **On Monday, 5 children were sick. On Friday, 1 child was sick. Which sentence is true?**

○ Fewer children were sick on Friday.

○ More children were sick on Friday.

○ Fewer children were sick on Monday.

5. **How many ounces heavier was the kitten on April 22 than on April 8?**

Weight of Kitten	
Date	Weight
April 8	12 ounces
April 15	15 ounces
April 22	17 ounces

○ 4 ounces

○ 5 ounces

○ 9 ounces

6. **How did the number of people change from 4:00 to 7:00?**

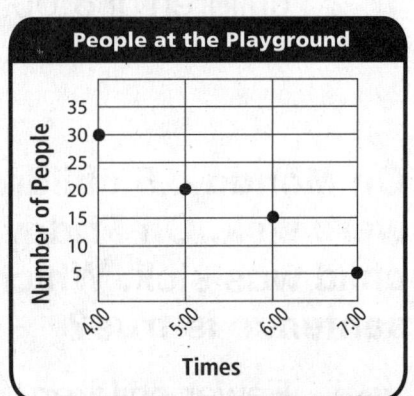

○ The number of people was less at 4:00.

○ The number of people was more at 7:00.

○ The number of people was less at 7:00.

7. **Use the graph.**

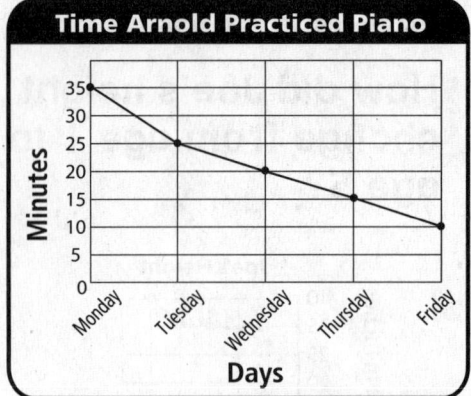

Tell how the data in the line graph changed over time.

_____

_____

_____

8. **Josie spent 15 minutes on her homework on Monday and 30 minutes on her homework on Tuesday. How many more minutes did Josie spend on her homework on Tuesday than on Monday?**

_____ more minutes

DAP1 Pose questions, use observations, interviews, and surveys to collect data, and organize data in charts, picture graphs and bar graphs.

1. Which survey question did you ask to get the data in the tally table?

Ways to Get to School	
Way	Tally
bus	卌 II
walk	IIII
bike	卌 IIII

○ What is your favorite way to get to school?

○ Do you like the bus?

○ What way do you ride your bike to school?

2. Each ☺ in a picture graph stands for 5 children. How many ☺ should you draw to show 15 children?

○ 2 ☺

○ 3 ☺

○ 5 ☺

3. Libby used the data in the tally chart to make a bar graph.

Hours We Read This Week	
Children	Tally
Marti	卌 I
Shantel	卌 II
Lee	卌 III

Which bar graph did she make?

○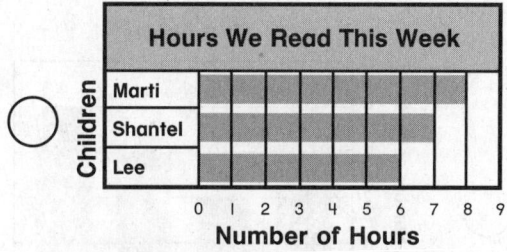

○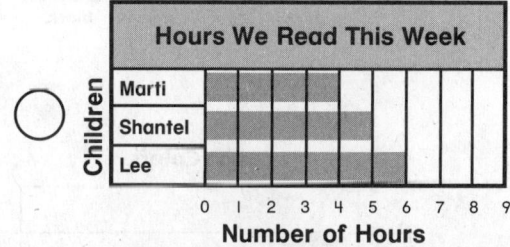

○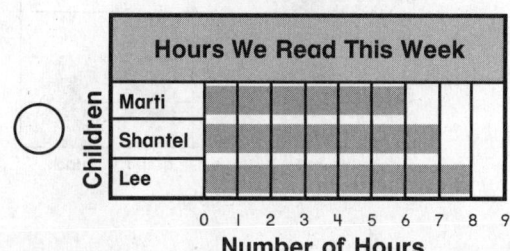

4. **Doug counts his shirts. He has 3 red shirts, 4 blue shirts, 2 green shirts, and 3 black shirts. He makes a bar graph to show how many of each color shirt he has. Which shows Doug's bar graph?**

○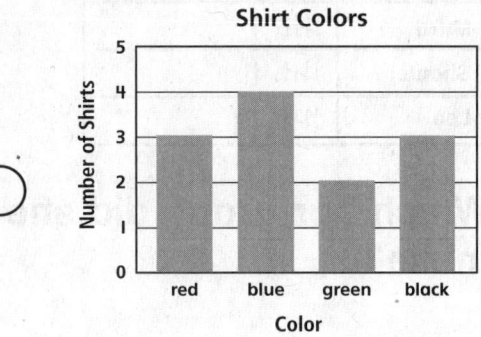

○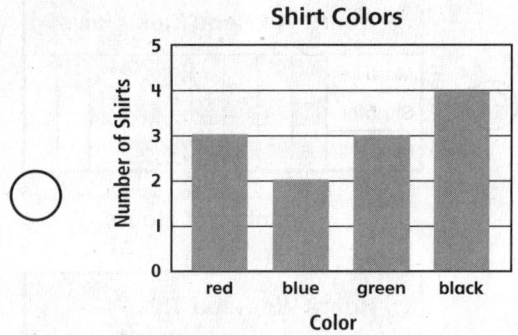

○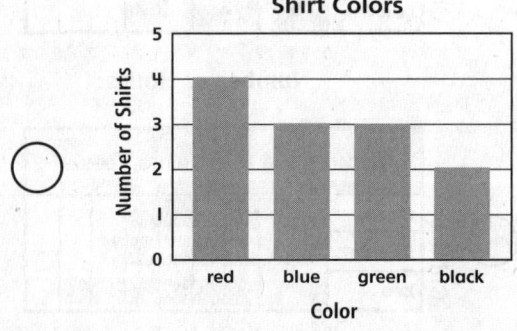

5. **Look at the tally table.**

Favorite Pets

Pet	Number of Children
dog	ⵏⵏⵏ |||
cat	ⵏⵏⵏ	

Use the tally table to make a picture graph. Draw a ☺ for every 2 children.

Favorite Pets	
dog	
cat	

Key: Each ☺ = 2 children.

6. **Write a survey question you could ask to find your friends' favorite colors.**

_____

_____

_____

⬤DAP2 **Read, interpret and make comparisons and predictions from data represented in charts, line plots, picture graphs and bar graphs.**

1. **Use the picture graph.**

Favorite Fruits				
Apple	☺			
Strawberry	☺	☺	☺	
Banana	☺	☺	☺	☺

Key: Each ☺ stands for 2 children.

How many children chose banana?

◯ 3 children

◯ 4 children

◯ 8 children

2. **The table shows the tiles in Terry's bag.**

Tiles in a Bag	
Color	**Number**
red	7
orange	3
black	6

Which color is Terry <u>most likely</u> to pull?

◯ red

◯ orange

◯ black

3. **How many more children chose grape than orange?**

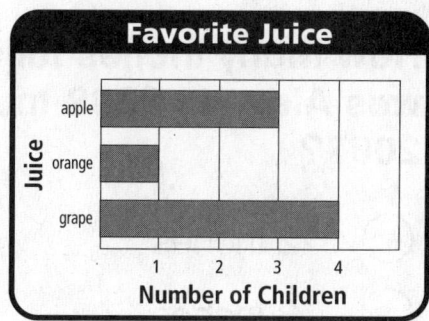

◯ 2 more children

◯ 3 more children

◯ 4 more children

4. **What number of pets do the <u>fewest</u> children have?**

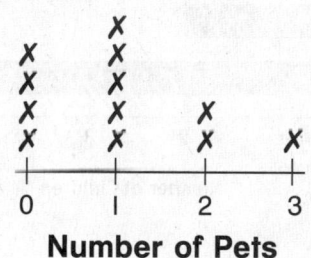

◯ 1 pet

◯ 2 pets

◯ 3 pets

5.

Alexa's Height	
Year	Height
2007	37 inches
2008	39 inches
2009	40 inches

How many inches taller was Alexa in 2009 than in 2007?

◯ 2 inches

◯ 3 inches

◯ 6 inches

6. **Which color did the <u>most</u> children choose?**

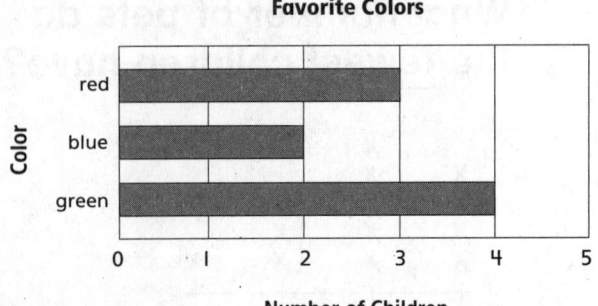

Favorite Colors

Number of Children

◯ red

◯ blue

◯ green

7. **Matt made a picture graph of marbles in a bag.**

Marbles in a Bag	
red	◯◯◯◯◯
green	◯◯
blue	◯◯◯

Key: Each ◯ = 2 marbles.

Which color of marble is Matt <u>least likely</u> to pull?

_____

8. **Use the bar graph.**

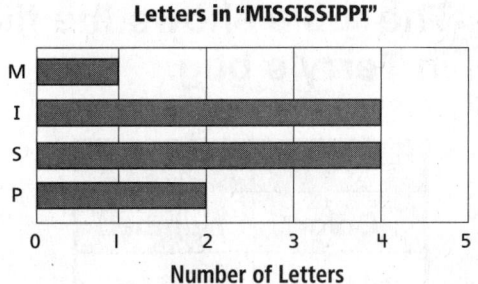

Letters in "MISSISSIPPI"

Number of Letters

How many more S's are there than P's?

_____ more S's

DAP3 Read and construct simple timelines to sequence events.

1. **At what time would you most likely eat lunch?**

- ○ 11:30 p.m.
- ○ 11:30 a.m.
- ○ 6:00 p.m.

2. **Look at the point on the timeline. Which would you most likely do at that time?**

8:30 a.m.   11:30 a.m.   2:30 p.m.   5:30 p.m.

- ○ go to school
- ○ go to sleep
- ○ eat dinner

3. **Which would you most likely do at 3:30 a.m.?**

be at school

brush your teeth

○

sleep

4. **At what time would you most likely do your homework?**

- ○ 4:00 p.m.
- ○ 4:00 a.m.
- ○ 12:00 p.m.

5. **Which would you most likely do at 9:00 a.m.?**

○

wait for bus

○

come home
from school

○

practice piano

6. **Look at the point on the timeline. Which would you most likely do at that time?**

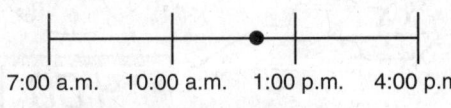

7:00 a.m.   10:00 a.m.   1:00 p.m.   4:00 p.m.

○ make lunch

○ eat dinner

○ go to sleep

7. **Write the time. Then circle a.m. or p.m.**

1:00

a.m.   p.m.

play outside

8. **Circle what you would most likely do at 5:30 p.m.**

help make dinner

go to music class

sleep

Name _____

Standards Practice

DAP4 Write a few sentences to describe and compare categories of data represented in a chart or graph, and make statements about the data as a whole.

1. Rita went into the butterfly garden at the zoo. She made a bar graph to show the different color butterflies she saw.

Colors of Butterflies

Color	Number of Butterflies
blue	
yellow	
orange	

0 1 2 3 4 5
Number of Butterflies

Which sentence is true?

○ Rita saw more orange than yellow butterflies.

○ Rita saw more blue than orange butterflies.

○ Rita saw more yellow butterflies than blue butterflies.

2. Jill collected the rainfall near her house. She made a table to show how much it rained each month.

Rainfall at Jill's House

Month	Amount of Rain
May	5 inches
June	4 inches
July	2 inches
August	3 inches

How many more inches did it rain in May than in July?

○ It rained 2 more inches.

○ It rained 3 more inches.

○ It rained 4 more inches.

Standards Practice
© Houghton Mifflin Harcourt. All rights Reserved.

141 Ohio Mathematics Achievement Test Practice

3. **Mr. Baxter counted the number of watches he sold at his store each month. He used the data to make a table.**

Watches Sold at a Store	
Month	**Number**
March	62
April	51
May	47
June	42

How did the number of watches the store sold change from March to June?

○ The store sold fewer watches in June.

○ The store sold more watches in June.

○ The store sold fewer watches in March.

4. **How many more dogs did Caden see at the park than J.T.?**

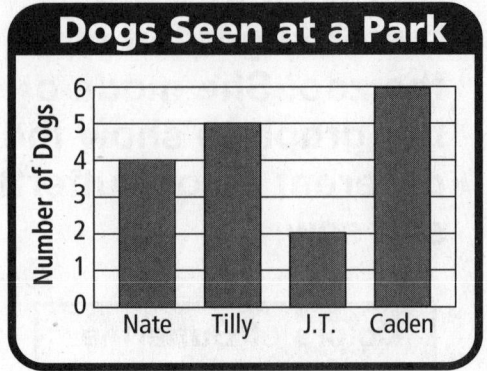

_____ more dogs

5. **Tell how the distance Selma ran changed from July 1 to July 22.**

Distances Selma Ran	
Date	**Distance**
July 1	1 mile
July 8	2 miles
July 15	3 miles
July 22	4 miles

_____

_____

_____

DAP5 **Identify untrue or inappropriate statements about a given set of data.**

1. **Annie, Brett, and Sara made a bar graph to show how many pencils each child has in his or her backpack.**

Pencils in Our Backpacks

Child	
Annie	
Brett	
Sara	

Number of Pencils: 0 1 2 3 4

Which sentence about the bar graph is not true?

○ Brett has more pencils than Annie.

○ Annie has more pencils than Sara.

○ Sara has fewer pencils than Brett.

2. **Samantha measured how much snow fell in her town. She made a table to show the amount of snowfall from January to April.**

Snowfall in Samantha's Town	
Month	Amount of Snow
January	6 inches
February	8 inches
March	2 inches
April	0 inches

Which sentence about Samantha's graph is true?

○ It snowed more inches in April than in March.

○ It snowed fewer inches in January than in February.

○ It snowed more inches in March than in February.

3. Which statement is <u>not</u> true?

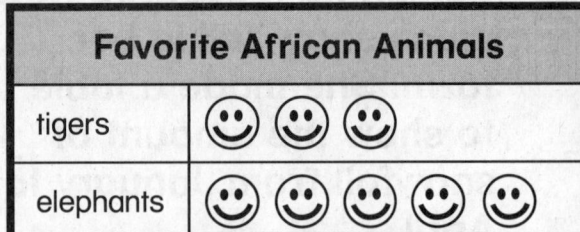

Favorite African Animals	
tigers	😊 😊 😊
elephants	😊 😊 😊 😊 😊

Key: Each 😊 = 2 children.

○ Five children chose elephants.

○ Six children chose tigers.

○ More children chose elephants then tigers.

4. Which statement is true?

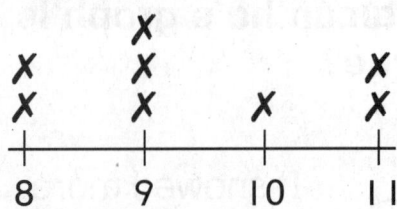

Number of Markers

○ The most children have 8 markers.

○ The most children have 9 markers.

○ The most children have 10 markers.

5. Write a true sentence about the bar graph.

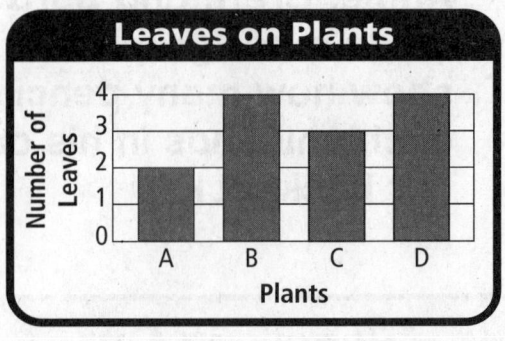

_____

_____

_____

6. Write a true sentence about the picture graph.

Favorite Kind of Juice	
orange	😊 😊 😊 😊
apple	😊 😊 😊

Key: Each 😊 = 2 children.

_____

_____

_____

DAP7 **List some of the possible outcomes of a simple experiment, and predict whether given outcomes are more, less or equally likely to occur.**

1. **Nick will spin the spinner one time.**

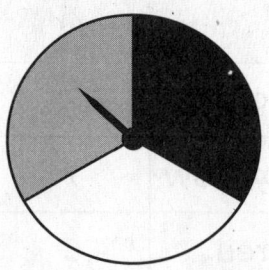

Which can Nick predict about the spin?

○ It is certain that the spin will be white.

○ It is possible that the spin will be black.

○ It is impossible that the spin will be gray.

2. **A bag has 5 yellow cubes, 3 blue cubes, 7 green cubes, and 3 red cubes. Which colors are equally likely to be pulled from the bag?**

○ blue and red

○ blue and yellow

○ green and yellow

3. **Wanda has a bag with gray cubes and white cubes. It is more likely that she will pull a gray cube from her bag than a white cube. Which might be Wanda's bag?**

○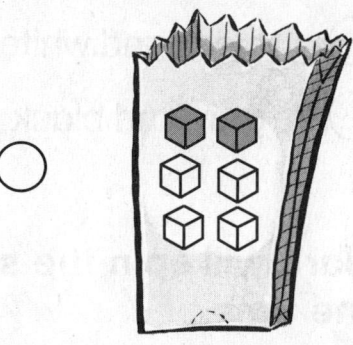

○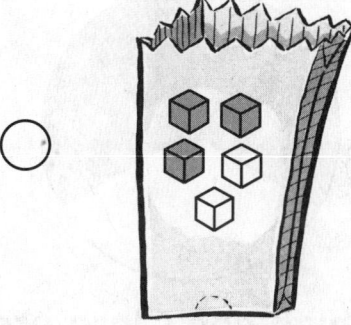

○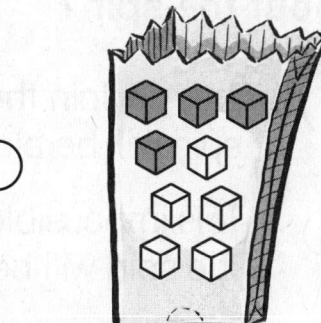

4. **What are the possible outcomes of the spinner?**

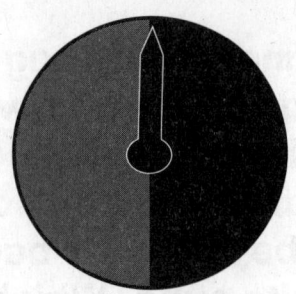

  ◯ gray and white

  ◯ black and white

  ◯ gray and black

5. **Clara will spin the spinner one time.**

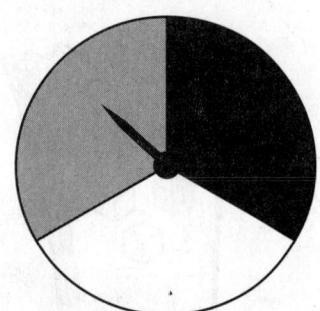

Which can Clara predict about the spin?

  ◯ It is certain that the spin will be black.

  ◯ It is impossible that the spin will be gray.

  ◯ It is possible that the spin will be white.

6. **Mike has a bag of marbles. He made a table to show the number of marbles in the bag.**

Marbles in a Bag

Color	Number
green	2
yellow	7
red	6

Which color marble is Mike <u>least likely</u> to pull?

_____

7. **Gary has a bag with gray and white cubes. Is he more likely to pull a gray cube or a white cube?**

Gary is more likely to pull a _____ cube.

DAP8 Use physical models and pictures to represent possible arrangements of 2 or 3 objects.

1. Frank makes outfits with 1 pair of pants and 2 shirts.

Which shows all the different outfits he can make?

2. Gwen has 2 kinds of jelly. She also has 2 kinds of peanut butter. She uses 1 kind of jelly and 1 kind of peanut butter for each sandwhich.

How many different kinds of sandwiches can Gwen make?

3. Sean can have a glass of milk or a glass of juice. He can also have some grapes or a granola bar.

How many different ways can he have a drink and a snack?

○ 2 ways

○ 3 ways

○ 4 ways

4. **Jared has 1 white block and 1 gray block.**

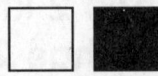

Which shows all the different ways Jared can put 1 block on top of the other?

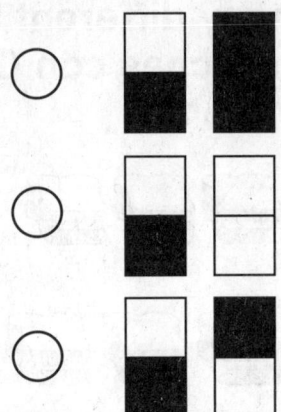

5. **Jason has 2 kinds of socks and 2 kinds of shoes.**

Jason wants to wear 1 kind of sock and 1 kind of shoe. How many different ways can he wear his socks and shoes?

○ 3 different ways

○ 4 different ways

○ 5 different ways

6. **Katie makes outfits with shirts and skirts.**

Draw all the different outfits Katie can make.

7. **Walt is choosing snacks for his lunch. He may choose any 2 of the 3 snacks.**

Draw all the different ways he can choose 2 of the snacks.

Addition and Subtraction to 18

1. Meg sees 4 butterflies on a bush.
   Then she sees 7 butterflies in a tree.
   How many butterflies does Meg see in all?

$$4 + 7 = \boxed{}$$

_____ butterflies

2. What is the difference?

$$15 - 6 = \boxed{}$$

3. What is the sum?

$$8 + 7 = \boxed{}$$

4. Jim has 17 marbles.
   He gives 5 of the marbles to Cody.
   How many marbles does Jim have left?
   Write the number sentence. Solve.

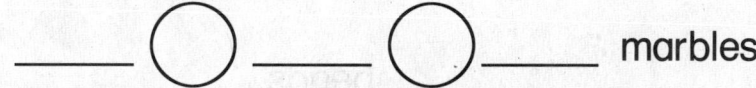 marbles

5. Marks sees 9 ducks on the pond.
He sees 3 more ducks in the air.
How many ducks does Mark see in all?
Write the number sentence. Solve.

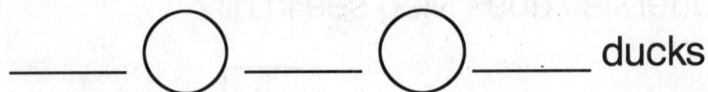

_____ ◯ _____ ◯ _____ ducks

---

6. What is the difference?

$$13 - 6 = \boxed{}$$

---

7. Jake makes 12 paper airplanes.
He gives 7 of them away.
How many paper airplanes does Jake have left?
Write the number sentence. Solve.

_____ ◯ _____ ◯ _____ paper airplanes

---

8. Lynn has 7 beads.
Her sister gives her 6 more beads.
How many beads does Lynn have now?

$$7 + 6 = \boxed{}$$

_____ beads

Count Coin Collections

1. What is the total value?

_____ ¢

2. Mathew has these coins.
What is the total value of the coins?

_____ ¢

3. What is the total value?

_____ ¢

4. Clara saves her coins. She has:

  2 quarters   3 dimes   1 nickel   3 pennies

  How much money does Clara have?

_____ ¢

---

5. What is the total value?

_____ ¢

---

6. Write the total value of each group.
Then write >, <, or =.

_____ ◯ _____

Patterns

1. Melissa makes a pattern.
   Draw the shape that comes next.

2. Draw the missing piece in the pattern.

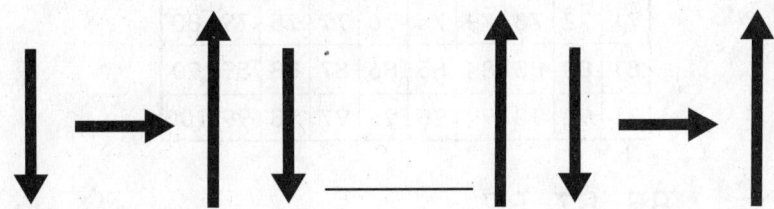

3. Skip-count by threes.
   Extend the pattern.

   3, 6, 9, _____, _____, _____

4. Carl uses letters to make a pattern.
   Circle the pattern unit.

   A A X A A X A A X

5. Tia makes a pattern.
Draw what comes next in Tia's pattern.

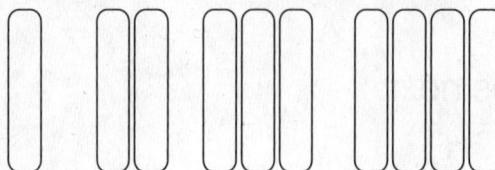 _____

6. Use the hundred chart.
Skip-count by twos.
Extend the pattern.

71	72	73	74	75	76	77	78	79	80
81	82	83	84	85	86	87	88	89	90
91	92	93	94	95	96	97	98	99	100

85, 87, 89, _____ , _____ , _____

7. Bob puts 10 toys in each bag.
How many toys are in 6 bags?
Complete the table to solve.

number of bags	1	2	3	4	5	6
number of toys	10	20	30			

There are _____ toys in 6 bags.

8. Circle the pattern unit.

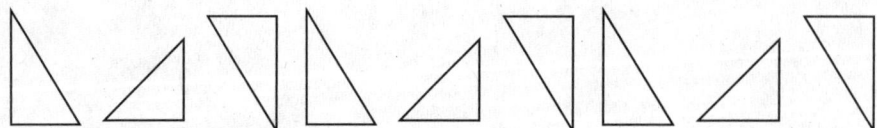

Two-Dimensional Shapes

1. Pam has a rectangle. Draw what Pam's shape might look like.

---

2. Draw an X on each triangle.

---

3. Kara cuts the paper shape along the dotted line.
   What new shapes does Kara make?

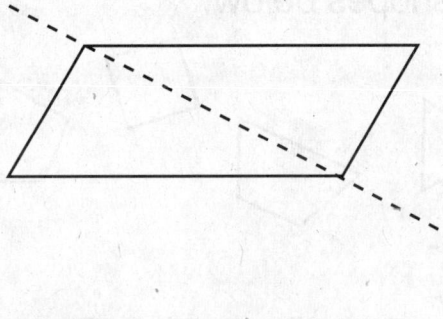

---

4. Tim has a circle. Draw what Tim's shape might look like.

5. Carlos has the shapes below.

He combines the shapes to make a new shape.
Circle the shape that Carlos might make.

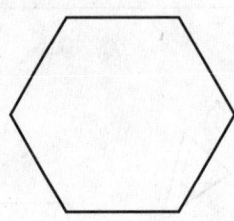 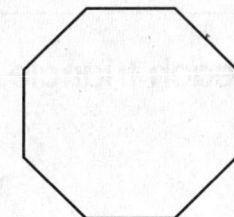

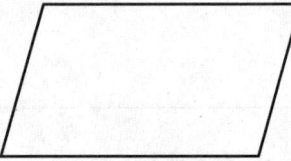 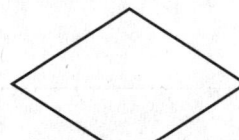

---

6. Jimmy draws the shapes below.

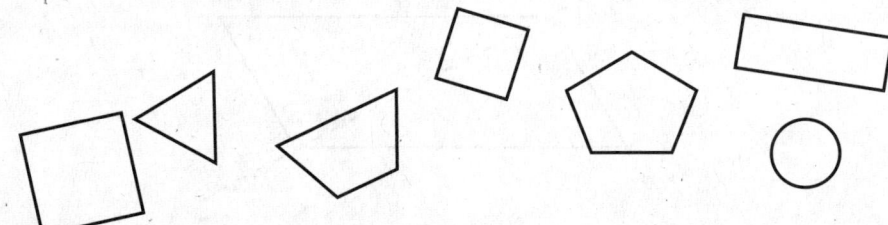

How many squares does Jimmy draw?

_____ squares

---

7. What is the name of this shape?

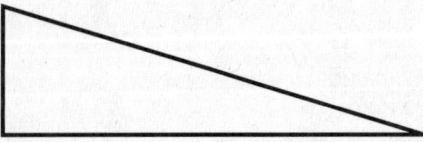 _____

Time to 5 Minutes

I. Write the time.

 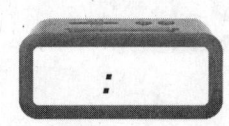

2. Bill starts piano practice at 5:45.
Piano practice ends at 6:30.
For how long is Bill at piano practice?

Start   Finish

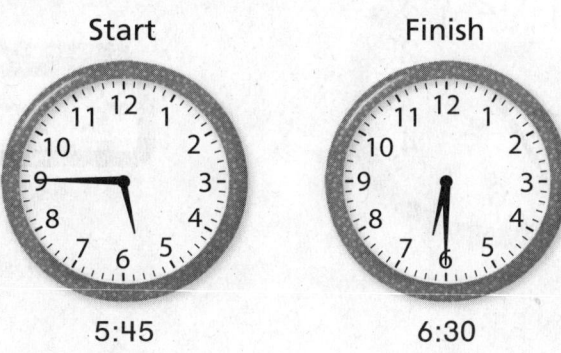

5:45   6:30

Bill is at piano practice for _____.

3. Write the time.

4. Draw the minute hand to show the same time.

5. Write the time.

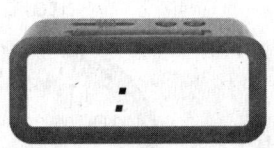

6. Alex gets on the bus at 8:55.
Draw the minute hand to show the time.

Lebanon Mason Monroe Railroad

You can ride on old trains and learn about train history at the Lebanon Mason Monroe Railroad. A one-hour ride takes you through Warren County in southwestern Ohio.

Many of the train cars the Railroad uses were built in the 1930s.

1. Car #101 has 72 seats. Car #104 has 54 seats. How may more seats are in Car #101 than Car #104?

_____

2. If 58 seats are taken in Car #101, how many seats are empty?

_____

3. Car #101 and Car #104 once carried passengers from home to work. One trip was about 42 miles. Today, the train takes a trip that is about 4 miles. How much longer was the original trip than the trip today?

_____

The Lebanon Mason Monroe Railroad has an open-air train car called a gondola. Gondola cars were once used to carry goods from one city to another. The Railroad has made changes to the car so that people can sit in it.

4. The Railroad put benches in the gondola. There is enough space for 20 people to sit. If 13 people sit in the car, how many seats are empty?

_____

_____

5. The Lebanon Mason Monroe Railroad has 25 miles of track. If the normal tour travels on only 4 miles of track, how much track is left?

_____

_____

6. The train passes a heron bird nest. If one of the people on the train counts 26 herons when the train passes and another person counts 17 herons, how many more herons did the first person see?

_____

_____

7. The Railroad's train goes 10 miles per hour. If the average speed of a train today is 48 miles per hour, how much faster does the newer train travel?

_____

Cleveland Museum of Natural History

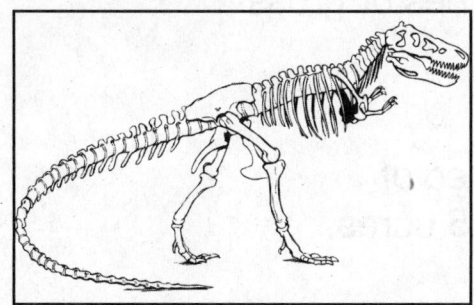

The Cleveland Museum of Natural History is filled with all kinds of science and nature for you to learn about. It has dinosaur skeletons, a wildlife center, and even a planetarium.

1. There is a new *Triceratops* skeleton at the museum. *Triceratops* was one of the biggest dinosaurs of its time, second only to *T. rex*. The skull alone is 9 feet long! If the skull is 9 feet long and the body is 12 feet long, what is the total length of the skeleton?

_____

_____

2. If 72 people came to see one planetarium show and 67 people came to see the next planetarium show, how many people came to both shows total?

_____

_____

3. At the museum's Wildlife Center, there are 15 kinds of frogs and 25 kinds of salamanders. How many kinds of frogs and salamanders are there in all?

_____

The museum has a wildlife center and nature areas where you can see animals from northern Ohio. There are many different kinds of animals at the nature center, so the nature areas are different, too. Some of the areas are filled with trees or grass. Others are filled with sand.

4. The Scheele Preserve Nature Area has an area of 28 acres. Woodford Woods has an area of 25 acres. How many acres are both areas combined?

_____

_____

5. The museum has an exhibit about Balto. Balto was a sled dog that helped deliver important medicine to the town of Nome, Alaska. Balto's journey saved many people. If Balto and his team traveled 21 miles, rested, and then traveled 32 miles more, how many miles did they travel in all?

_____

_____

6. The museum has a program called Natural Melodies. Music students write songs just for the museum. If one of these songs is 17 minutes long and another is 11 minutes long, how long are both songs in all?

_____

Cincinnati Zoo

The Cincinnati Zoo is the country's second-oldest zoo. The zoo has over 500 animals.

Ellen went to the Cincinnati Zoo with her class. She wanted to know which animals the children in her class liked. She asked them to choose a favorite then made this bar graph.

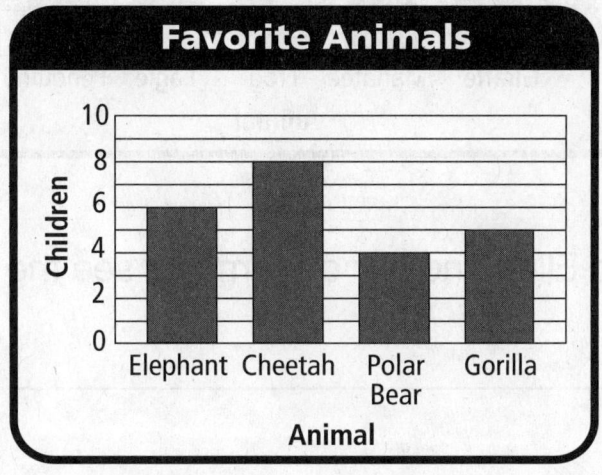

1. How many children chose the gorilla? _____

2. How many more children chose the elephant than the polar bear? _____

3. Which animal got the most votes?

Ellen and her classmates counted the animals they saw in the park. Then they made this bar graph to show how many of each kind of animal they saw.

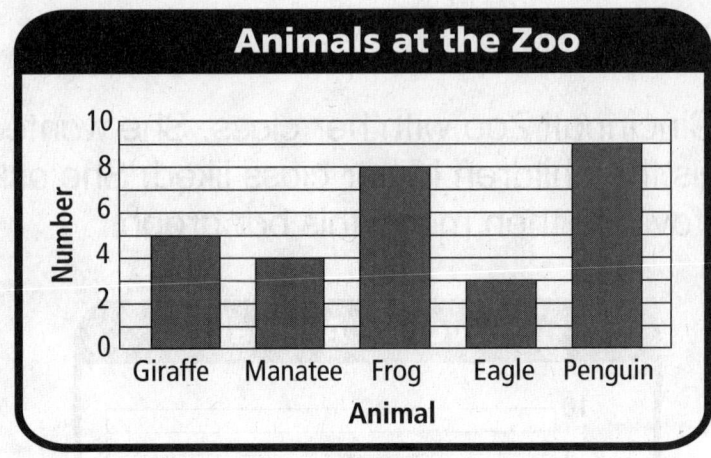

4. Which animal did Ellen and her classmates see the most?

_____

5. Which animal did the children see twice as many of, than the manatee?

_____

6. How many more frogs did the children see than giraffes?

_____

Van Buren State Park

Van Buren State Park is in northwest Ohio. It was named after Martin Van Buren, who was the 8th President of the United States. The land in the park was set aside for animals and nature.

1. Ron and his class went on a field trip to Van Buren State Park. On a hike, Ron saw 3 squirrels and 2 raccoons. What fraction of the animals that Ron saw were raccoons?

$$\frac{}{}$$

2. Ron's class has 18 children. If 10 children want to go horseback riding, what fraction of the children in Ron's class want to go horseback riding?

$$\frac{}{}$$

Van Buren State Park has a nature center that does programs for children. One program is an Owl Prowl. Children meet at the nature center to learn about owls then go out to find them in the park.

3. Carrie went on the Owl Prowl. She counted all of the owls she saw. Carrie saw 7 owls total. If 4 of those owls were screech owls, what fraction of the owls Carrie saw were screech owls?

_____

4. Van Buren State Park has a butterfly gazebo. If Carrie sees 4 yellow butterflies and 4 orange butterflies, what fraction of the butterflies are orange?

_____

5. There are 6 miles of hiking trails. If Carrie walks for 2 miles, what fraction of the hiking trails did she walk?

_____

Number, Number Sense and Operations

Count on to find the **sum**.

1. 6
   + 3

2. 1
   + 8

3. 10
   + 3

Count back to find the **difference**.

4. 9
   − 3

5. 6
   − 2

6. 7
   − 2

Add or **subtract**. **Regroup** if you need to.

7. 31
   + 25

8. 24
   + 59

Compare. Write <, >, or =.

15. 518 ◯ 728

16. 476 ◯ 439

17. 254 ◯ 259

18. 934 ◯ 934

Name ____________________

Vocabulary Practice

Round to the nearest 10.

1. 22 ______

2. 67 ______

3. 91 ______

4. 55 ______

5. 33 ______

6. 86 ______

7. 8 ______

8. 45 ______

Circle the value of the underlined digit.

9. 32<u>8</u>

8 80 800

10. <u>4</u>91

4 40 400

11. 5<u>5</u>3

5 50 500

12. 20<u>2</u>

2 20 200

13. 6<u>7</u>4

7 70 700

14. <u>9</u>26

9 90 900

Measurement

1. Use an **inch** ruler to **measure**.

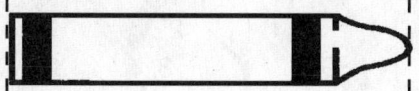 _____ inches

2. Use a **centimeter** ruler to **measure**.

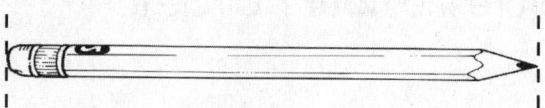 _____ centimeters

Choose the unit you would use to measure each.

3.

inch   yard

4.

quart   cup

5.

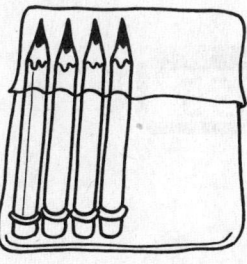

gram   kilogram

6.

pound   ounce

1. Which clock shows 8 o'clock? Circle it.

2. Which clock shows 30 minutes before the **hour**? Circle it.

3. Which clock shows 15 minutes after the **hour**? Circle it.

| 9:30 | 5:00 | 7:15 |

4. Draw the **minute** hand.

| 6:20 | 12:35 | 1:55 |

Geometry and Spatial Sense

Circle the word that names each picture.

1.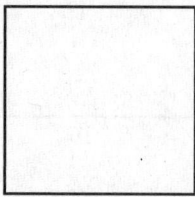

circle   square

2.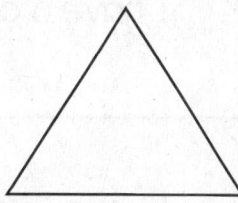

cone   triangle

3.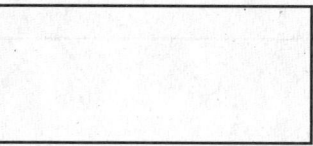

rectangle   cylinder

4.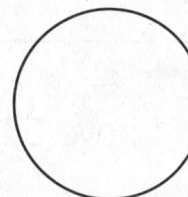

circle   rectangle

Name each figure.

| hexagon | octagon | pentagon | trapezoid |

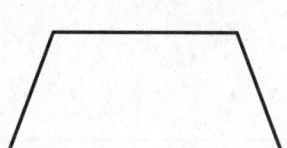 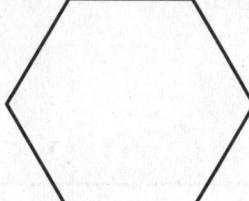 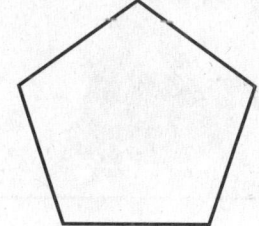

5. _____

6. _____

7. _____

Look at the solid figure.
Circle the correct sentence.

1.    I have no faces, no edges, and no vertices.

   I have a circle as a face.

2.    I have 5 faces, 8 edges, and 5 vertices.

   I have 6 faces that are triangles.

3.    I have 5 faces.

   I have 6 faces, 12 edges, and 8 vertices.

4.    I have 6 square faces.

   I have 5 faces, 8 edges, and 5 vertices.

5.    I am a cylinder.

   I am a cone.

6.    I am a sphere.

   I am a cylinder.

Patterns, Functions and Algebra

1. Circle the correct **pattern unit** for the pattern.

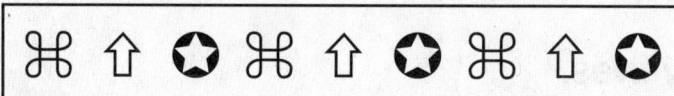

Circle the **pattern unit** to predict what comes next.
Continue the **repeating pattern.**

2. ◯ ○ ○ ◯ ○ ○ ○ ◯ ○ ___ ___

3. △ △ ▷ △ △ ▷ △ ___ ___

4. ▯ ▭ ▯ ▯ ▭ ▯ ▯ ___ ___

5. ▢ △ ▷ ▢ ___ ___ ▢ △ ▷

1. **Skip count** by twos.

18, 20, 22, _____, _____, _____, _____

2. **Skip count** by fives.

36, 41, 46, _____, _____, _____, _____

3. Write a **rule** for the **pattern**.

32, 30, 28, 26, 24

Subtract _____.

4. Write the missing number in the **pattern**.

3, 6, 9, _____, 15, _____, 21, 24

5. Follow the **rule**. Find the missing number.

Add 8.

In	Out
4	12
5	___
6	14

Data Analysis and Probability

Dean pulled a handful of coins out of a bag.
He recorded what he pulled out in the **tally table**.

Coins in the Handful

Coin	Tally
quarter	III
nickel	I
penny	IIII III

1. Make a **bar graph**. Use the information from the tally table.

Coins in the Handful										
quarter										
nickel										
penny										

0   1   2   3   4   5   6   7   8   9   10

Use the **bar graph**. Make a prediction about
each **outcome**.

2. Which coin is Dean **most likely** to pull from the bag?

_____

3. Which coin is Dean **least likely** to pull from the bag?

_____

Tell whether each event is **certain** or **impossible**.

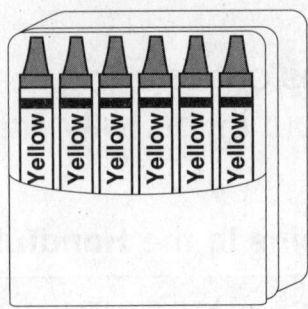

1. A red crayon is picked. _____

2. A yellow crayon is picked. _____

3. A blue crayon is picked. _____

Answer the question.

4. List all the **possible outcomes**. _____

_____

Tell whether each event is **certain** or **impossible**.

5. A block is picked. _____

6. A marble is picked. _____

Inch and Centimeter Rulers

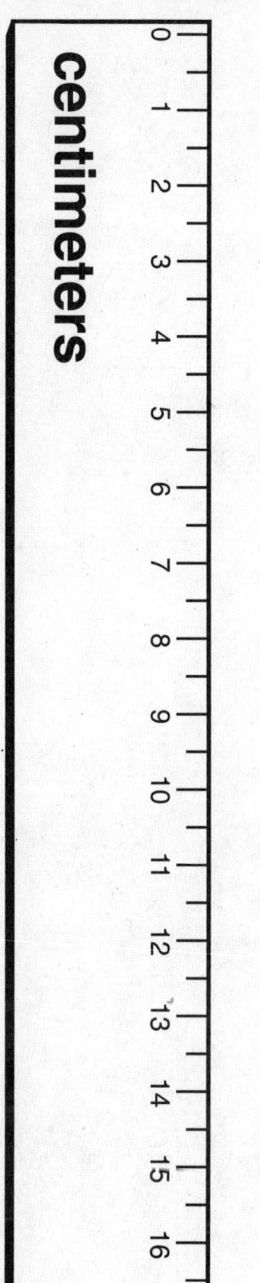

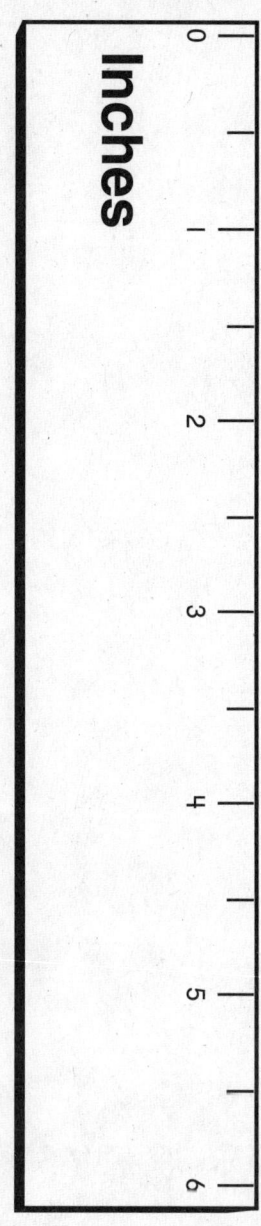